The
Art of
Creative
Thinking

The Art of Creative Thinking

89 Ways to See Things Differently

Rod Judkins

A Perigee Book

PERIGEE

An imprint of Penguin Random House LLC
375 Hudson Street, New York, New York 10014

Copyright © 2016 by Rod Judkins

Illustrations by the author.

LIBRARY OF CONGRESS CATALOGING-IN-PUBLICATION DATA

Judkins, Rod, author.
The art of creative thinking : 89 ways to see things
differently / Rod Judkins.—First edition.
pages cm
ISBN 978-0-399-17683-8 (paperback)
1. Creative thinking—Miscellanea.   I. Title.
BF408.J83 2016
153.3'5—dc23   2015031773

First edition: March 2016

PRINTED IN THE UNITED STATES OF AMERICA

1   3   5   7   9   10   8   6   4   2

Text design by Elke Sigal

Most Perigee books are available at special quantity discounts for bulk purchases for sales promotions, premiums, fund-raising, or educational use. Special books, or book excerpts, can also be created to fit specific needs. For details, write: SpecialMarkets@ penguinrandomhouse.com.

Introduction

When I first stepped into an art college as a student, I instantly felt at home—for the first time ever.

At school prior to that, creativity had been suppressed and crushed. It was something that teachers and authorities actually feared. They regarded it as dangerous, something they couldn't control. They steered students away from it in the same way they steered them away from drugs, burglary and gambling.

At art college I found the opposite. The spirit was one in which mistakes were good. Where you could try and fail. There was no emphasis on getting it "right." All around me were people experimenting for the sheer hell of it, doing things that made no sense—or rather doing things *because* they made no sense. There was an air of freedom and release. Meanwhile, in the world outside, people were being thoughtlessly reasonable, doing something because it was what everyone else was doing. Paradoxically, the creative thinking of art college led to more worthwhile accomplishments than the logical, sensible approach. Many years later, when I returned to art education as a university lecturer, I found the environment to be the same.

Since emerging from art college all those years ago, I've balanced various roles—as an educator, artist, writer, adviser and speaker—and have also become a hunter-gatherer of creative techniques. After leaving the Royal College of Art, I had numerous solo exhibitions of my paintings. I have exhibited in many countries, and also at Tate Britain, the Royal Academy and the National Portrait Gallery. I've taught at Central Saint Martins College of Art since 1999 and am also a creative consultant, working with companies and businesses around the world, delivering workshops that solve professional problems using creativity as the key. The workshops reveal useful techniques that access original ideas and help people and businesses develop a more direct relationship to their own creativity.

I care passionately about taking the spirit of creativity that exists in the art world out into the wider world. I didn't write *The Art of Creative Thinking* because I wanted to. I wrote it because it was needed. In my many years helping students, businesses and companies across various industries, and people in all fields, from scientists to office workers, I have seen firsthand how thinking creatively can transform everyday life. I've shown how the principles of jazz improvisation could make an admin office run more smoothly, how to help an entrepreneur whose scuba-diving company was facing bankruptcy because sharks had infested the area (long story short: we made this his unique selling point) and helped a company to sell their designer furniture by promoting it as uncomfortable.

This book is intended to be an overview of many useful

creative-thinking techniques, and an examination of the thought processes and methods creative people use and which can be used to help everyone. But I also want to share stories of some of the inevitable obstacles that aspiring creative thinkers encounter and the methods they use to overcome them. These are challenges that all of us face in day-to-day life, whatever our career or field of expertise: anxiety that we have no special talents; the absence of any burning, driving passion; craving success in an area we're not actually any good at; being unable to make a living from our true passion; having too many other responsibilities and commitments; feeling either too young or too old, too naïve or too jaded.

This book is not meant to be read in a linear way. When your creativity is running low or you feel the need for inspiration, open it to any page at random.

The Art of Creative Thinking began as a tribute to what all of us can learn from art school, but what I hope to show more than anything is that thinking creatively is not a *professional* activity—it's a way of relating to your life. Creativity is not about creating a painting, novel or house but about creating *yourself*, creating a better future and taking the opportunities that you are currently missing.

See what happens when you make something happen

On the classic TV game show *What's My Line?* the blindfolded celebrity panelists interrogated a "mystery guest" in order to determine the guest's occupation. The guest was restricted to yes-or-no answers. In the most fascinating episode of the show, the panelists quickly became perplexed because the guest answered yes to almost every occupation they inquired about. They asked him if he was a writer and he answered yes. It was true; as well as three nonfiction books, he had written a novel, *Hidden Faces*. Asked if he was a performer: yes. Had he produced any pieces of performance art? Yes. At one point an exasperated panelist exclaimed, "There's nothing this man doesn't do!" The program descended into hilarious chaos.

The guest could also have said that he was a furniture maker; he designed many chairs, and his sofa of Mae West's lips became a design classic. As a filmmaker he created the groundbreaking *Un Chien Andalou* and *L'Age d'Or*. He also masterminded the ethereal dream sequence in Hitchcock's *Spellbound* and the unique short animated film *Destino* with Walt Disney. As a jewelry-maker he created intricate jewelry designs that often contained moving parts, such as the Royal Heart, made of gold and encrusted with rubies and diamonds, with a center beating like a real heart. As an architect he designed buildings, the most famous being his house in Port Lligat and his extraordinary Teatro Museo in Figueres. He wanted a house, so he made one—why let someone do it? He also designed theater sets, clothes, textiles and perfume bottles. He even created a person—Amanda Lear. He met her in a nightclub in 1965 when she was called Peki D'Oslo. He renamed her, reinvented her and spread mysterious stories about her, successfully launching her into the disco/art scene, which she then took by storm.

When the *What's My Line?* panelists lifted their blindfolds, the mystery guest was revealed—surrealist painter Salvador Dalí.

A creative mind always seeks to explore new areas. The manufacturer of Chupa Chups lollipops asked Dalí to design a new logo. He created a daisy insignia and lettering (still appearing on the candies today). Dalí even suggested the logo be on top of the wrapper so that it was always fully displayed—advice the manufacturer followed. It was one of the least significant works he created, but it is significant because it reveals his thinking. Dalí could have thought, "This isn't important enough. I'm a famous, wealthy artist who will appear in art history books," but he thought it sounded like fun so he gave it a go.

School and society often make us feel our abilities are

limited and rob us of our creative confidence. Although we are born with incredible imagination, intuition and intelligence, many people are trained not to use these powers, and as a result they wither. Our schools, families and friends project a limited view of our abilities onto us. If the creative want something, they go ahead and try. Not all of Dalí's designs, films and experiments in different mediums were a success, but enough worked for him to become respected.

Modern designers like Philippe Starck and Zaha Hadid also have a unique vision. They are famous for designing iconic opera houses, stadiums and hotels. They also design cars, bicycles, lamps, jewelry, chairs and boats. They developed a way of thinking that could be applied to any project. Sometimes you succeed and sometimes you fail, but it's important to try and see what happens.

A creative mindset can be applied to everything you do and enrich every aspect of your life. Creativity isn't a switch that's flipped on or off; it's a way of seeing, engaging with and responding to the world around you. The creative are creative when filing documents, cooking, arranging timetables or doing housework. Try to develop an alternative way of thinking that can be applied to any challenge or project, no matter how far out of your comfort zone.

I THINK ANY ACTOR WORTH THEIR SALT WANTS
TO SHOW AS MUCH VERSATILITY AS THEY
POSSIBLY CAN.

—*Daniel Radcliffe*

Agree? Venture beyond your comfort zone in the next chapter. Disagree? Discover why creativity and housework just don't go together on page 126.

be a beginner, forever

I had to create a new TV soap opera. I'd never done anything like that before. I was an artist, a painter, yet here I found myself, standing in front of thirty TV professionals. They were looking at me impatiently and expectantly.

I hadn't known what I was in for when I accepted the job. The Dubai TV station had asked me to deliver creative workshops that I had developed for my students at Central Saint Martins. CSM made them available to a wider audience. The TV station flew me to Dubai and showered me with luxury: a room in the Dubai Hilton, a driver and limo, expenses, the works. I felt obligated to them and had prepared thoroughly. I didn't want to go all that way and discover I'd left out something important.

They had rented a conference room in a five-star hotel for me to deliver my workshop. As I was led in to meet the production team, the manager turned to me and said, "Oh, by the way, instead of the workshops, we'd like you to help us create a new soap opera based in Dubai." It was a bombshell. My preparation had been wasted.

I stood in front of the eager production team. The room oozed wealth and opulence; embroidered tablecloths, ornate chairs and high-tech screens everywhere. I felt ill at ease. I was used to art studios with paint spatters on the walls, bare floors and a place where you could make mistakes with freedom. I gave a short talk about myself; in reality I was stalling for time, trying to work out what to do. I knew I couldn't produce anything creative in that room, yet they'd spent a fortune on it. I'd have to disrupt it. To the dismay of the hotel staff, I made them move all the tables and chairs out. I didn't want everyone sitting down feeling relaxed. With the room empty, I felt better. It was like a blank canvas to an artist or a blank sheet of paper to a writer. They all looked irritated, though.

The TV station was struggling to create a new soap opera because their ideas were predictable and dull. They wanted me to resurrect them. I said it would be easier to scrap their ideas and start fresh. Better to think new ideas than waste time trying to salvage old ones. They were annoyed by this.

The team of scriptwriters, cameramen, production staff,

soundmen, set designers, costume designers and more had attitudes that stifled creative thinking: "I have been doing this for years. I'm an expert. I have been trained to do this properly. I know exactly what I'm doing." They wanted to do things the way they had always done them. I knew I couldn't work with them until they opened their minds to new methods.

I swapped their roles. I asked the cameramen to write some script ideas, the costume designers to write up characters, the soundmen to think of locations and so on. They were furious.

I had to convince them to give it a try. Eventually they did. Fear of failure vanished because the weight of expectation had been lifted. They no longer had a reputation to protect because they were not doing what they'd been trained to do. They improvised. They played around. New, original ideas poured out. They had fun. They were liberated. We created some new scripts with exciting characters, unusual settings and innovative plotlines. They wanted to get actors to rehearse the roles and start filming "properly." I pointed out that that was what they usually did. Instead we filmed a rough episode with them acting the roles. They ad-libbed unusual and interesting ideas as we filmed.

They developed the rough ideas further after I'd returned to England. The soap went on air. It was unique and completely different for Dubai. The process had determined the end result.

Make the most of inexperience. A beginner has a fresh perspective. The amateurish and unprofessional are open to new ideas: they'll try anything. They don't know how things "should" be done, and haven't yet become entrenched in a particular method. Nothing is "wrong" for them because they don't know what is "right."

It's important to avoid becoming an expert, specialist or authority. An expert constantly refers to *past* experience. Whatever has worked in the past, the expert repeats. An expert turns knowledge into a repetitive ritual. His or her expertise becomes a straitjacket. Furthermore, experts claim to have many years' experience. What they actually have is one year's experience repeated many times. They see new methods as a threat to their expertise, and seek to stamp them out.

To breathe fresh air into yourself or your company, spend a day working on something that's valuable, but not what you're "supposed" to be working on. Switching jobs creates an environment that encourages innovation. Constantly search for new ways of doing the same things and do not repeat what you already know. Don't do things in the usual way; do them in the unusual way.

WHATEVER I KNOW HOW TO DO, I'VE ALREADY
DONE. THEREFORE I MUST ALWAYS DO WHAT I
DO NOT KNOW HOW TO DO.

—*Eduardo Chillida*

Inspired? Discover the self-taught architect on page 59. Uninspired? Copy John Cheever and imitate your idols on page 138.

blame michelangelo

The cult of the creative genius appeared with art's first superstar, Michelangelo. In 1550 his biographer and PR guru, Vasari, promoted the idea of the "Divine Michelangelo." His talent was a gift from God, Vasari said, and he claimed that God bestowed such ability only on the privileged few, the chosen ones. This notion fostered an elitist and disempowering attitude toward creativity.

What Vasari failed to mention was Michelangelo's reliance on an army of assistants. Archives contain hundreds of bills for his highly skilled helpers—a dozen worked continuously on the Sistine Chapel ceiling, for example, which explains the sheer scale of the achievement and the fact that this physical task might seem impossible for one man. For me, this does not belittle Michelangelo's achievement. His role was similar to that of a film director, like Francis Ford Coppola in today's world, someone who realizes an enormous project by guiding the technical crew to the fulfillment of that vision—an awesome achievement, but not a superhuman one. While the *Godfather* trilogy was Coppola's vision, and he got incredible performances out of Marlon Brando and the rest of the cast, it would be wrong to attribute the design of the costumes, the writing of the script, the arrangement of the lighting, the editing and everything else involved in the making of a film to the director.

Undoubtedly one of the world's great geniuses, Michelangelo had not so much a divine gift as an intensely nurtured talent. Brought up by quarrymen, he could chisel and cut blocks of stone from the age of six. By the age of twelve he had been carving stone for thousands of hours. At fourteen he was apprenticed to an artist's studio. That level of skilled training is not possible today. In fact, it's illegal.

The old masters are a great source of inspiration, but we cannot ever emulate their level of skill. We have to discover our own strengths. When I deliver creativity workshops to companies, I try to get everyone to take part: the accountants, admin staff, technicians—whoever is around, not just the "creatives." By the end of the sessions the "non-creatives" are surprised at how creative they are. They had been led to believe they didn't have the ability, and therefore they lacked the confidence. Creative thinking is like a muscle that needs to be strengthened through exercise. I often set exercises that each last five or ten minutes, just as an athlete might do a series of short workouts to stay fit.

How often have you heard "I can't draw to save my life" or "I'm tone-deaf"? The concept of innate talent erodes confidence. Many people don't develop their talents because they are made to feel they weren't born with the amount required to be truly great.

Creativity is more than just technical skill too. A creative mind communicates ideas in a fresh way. It's more interesting if an engineer builds a rocket from scrap metal, a painter uses maple syrup or a harpist plays a clothesline. Our task is to develop our creative potential in whatever forms it may take, whether we think we were "born" with it or not.

NOT EVERY PERSON HAS THE SAME KINDS OF
TALENTS, SO YOU DISCOVER WHAT YOURS ARE
AND WORK WITH THEM.

— Frank Gehry

Convinced? Discover what the Fab Four can tell you about talent versus effort in the next chapter. Not convinced? See if Picasso can persuade you on page 46.

be committed to commitment

I had never been so petrified. I didn't understand what was happening. I was a child of seven, and I clung to my aunt's jacket for fear of being swept away in the stampeding mob of screaming, wailing girls. The noise was deafening. It's impossible to describe the sheer magnitude of the hysteria. Girls fainted and collapsed, and paramedics rushed past holding their floppy, contorted bodies. It was like a medieval battlefield. I was crushed on all sides by a throng of thousands. Their eyes were wet with tears and their faces twisted with distress.

Then the Beatles stepped out of the plane and things went really crazy. It was 1964, and my aunt, who worked at Heathrow, had taken me to see the Fab Four return to England after a triumphant trip to the USA.

When the Beatles played on the legendary *Ed Sullivan Show* on TV, it was a milestone in American pop culture. A record-breaking audience of 73 million viewers was mesmerized.

To the USA, the Beatles were an overnight success, but in fact Lennon and McCartney had been playing together since 1957. In the clubs of Hamburg they performed/endured live nonstop shows for eight hours a day, seven days a week until two in the morning, and had to work incredibly hard to attract audiences from the many clubs in Hamburg competing for attention. Their abilities and confidence increased. By 1964 they had played roughly twelve hundred times, totaling thousands of hours' playing time, more than most rock bands play in their entire careers. Those hours of performing set the Beatles apart. They were addicted to practice, yet their rehearsing was not repetitive but adventurous. They didn't play the classic rock songs of the time over and over until they sounded exactly like the originals, as other bands did; they experimented and improvised, constantly embellishing the standards until they made them their own. They understood that there was nothing to be gained from mechanical repetition. The Beatles gave one another constant feedback, to improve and make their sound more and more like the Beatles and less and less like everyone else.

In their early days the Beatles were not great musicians; there were better, more technically proficient guitarists, singers and drummers. (John Lennon was once asked at a press conference if he thought Ringo was the best drummer in the world; he jokingly replied, "Ringo isn't the best drummer in the Beatles.") Yet on *The Ed Sullivan Show*, the four lads from the backstreets of Liverpool displayed no trace of nerves. Their confidence was the result of years of playing together and painstaking development.

Ninety-nine percent of the difference between successful innovative people and those who fail is commitment to self-improvement. The extraordinary amount of time and effort the successful put into developing their work amplifies their abilities. If someone is more successful than you, chances are they work harder at self-development. Practice is important, but it has to be *good* practice. Bad practice is thoughtlessly repeating something to perfect it. Good practice is putting time into imaginative improvement. When Matisse produced a series of paintings of the same female model, he didn't achieve more and more accuracy: he achieved more and more inventiveness.

The Beatles got the most out of their talent by investing the imaginative practice needed to develop their qualities. We only get out what we put in. No masterpieces have ever been produced by a talented but lazy artist.

A GENIUS! FOR THIRTY-SEVEN YEARS I'VE
PRACTICED FOURTEEN HOURS A DAY, AND NOW
THEY CALL ME A GENIUS!

— *Pablo de Sarasate*

Discover how two of the twentieth century's most accomplished musicians overcame unimaginable challenges on page 115, or why, like Beethoven, you should look forward to disappointment on page 133.

be the medium of your medium

Did the Space Shuttle *Columbia* break apart while reentering the Earth's atmosphere, instantly killing seven crew members, because of a poorly designed PowerPoint slide? During its launch, a few days earlier, a piece of insulation foam had struck the shuttle's wing. While *Columbia* was still orbiting the Earth, NASA engineers showed the results of their investigation to their superiors. The piece of foam was hundreds of times bigger than anything they had ever tested and could have caused a severe fracture. Unfortunately their warning was conveyed on PowerPoint. Their superiors walked away from the presentation thinking everything was fine.

Visually stunning presentations tell a story, engage their audience and make information meaningful, entertaining and beautiful. The sheer magnitude of the problem NASA was facing was lost. It was buried in a slide crowded with bullet points. Edward Tufte, a Yale University professor and researcher into the presentation of visual information, investigated the incident and demonstrated that PowerPoint encourages poor thinking by its very design. He criticized the format: complex ideas squashed into bulleted lists distorts the information. If the *Columbia* information had been presented in another medium, the disaster could almost certainly have been prevented. An independent board reached the same conclusion after reading Tufte's analysis, admitting that "It is easy to understand how a senior manager might read this PowerPoint slide and not realize that it addresses a life-threatening situation."

Your working environment, whether it's a supermarket, office, studio or building site, persuades you to work and think in certain ways. The more aware you are of that, and the more you understand your medium, the more you can use it to your advantage.

A meeting about finance is not about finance, it's about meetings: their format, internal politics, hierarchies and the way things are managed and governed. The most common decision at a meeting is to have another meeting.

Artists were the first to investigate this idea, in particular the surrealists. René Magritte's paintings were paintings about paintings. His surrealist ideas have had a profound influence on our understanding of how the medium transforms the message. Instead of producing art about something he had observed, his work reflected on what a painting was and the effect that it has on the viewer. He asked his audience to question the illusion they were presented with.

Magritte's painting *The Treachery of Images* showed a pipe with the words "This is not a pipe." This seems at first look like a contradiction, but is actually true: it is not a pipe, it is an image of a pipe. Magritte was pointing out that a painting is an illusion. He was trying to understand the language of painting, how it worked and how it conveyed ideas, and to challenge observers' preconditioned perceptions of the art form. A painting of flowers is not about flowers, it is about the medium of painting: the traditions, history, the frame, the gallery and the expectations the viewer has.

Artists like Magritte understood their medium and conveyed information that was visual poetry. That made it more memorable and easily understood, unlike the information from posters, television, newspapers and the Internet that we're bombarded by now. We're drowning in it. We are dazed by Power-Point presentations in which multiple bullet points are fired at us. Bullet points that can kill.

Most people are passive consumers who never analyze the medium. At the movies, most viewers go along with the illusion and enjoy the spectacle. For a creative thinker, though, the entertainment is in deconstructing the spectacle and imagining how it could have been done differently. What if the last scene and the first scene were swapped? What if the lead and one of the supporting actors changed roles? What if it were a silent movie? Imagining how the elements could be altered sharpens creative thinking and deepens your understanding.

THE NEW MEDIA ARE NOT BRIDGES BETWEEN
MAN AND NATURE: THEY ARE NATURE.

—*Marshall McLuhan*

Not tempted to become the medium of your medium? Try being your subject instead—from the inside out, on page 45.

don't be someone else

"In order to be irreplaceable one must always be different," said eccentric, pioneering French designer Coco Chanel. From the beginning of her career, Chanel defied convention. She didn't like the way women were forced to be uncomfortable to look fashionable. She didn't like corsets, so she replaced them with casual elegance and comfort. She was heavily attacked by the fashion press, but was unrepentant: "Luxury must be comfortable, otherwise it is not luxury." Her new vision made her one of the most important figures in the history of fashion. In the

1920s and '30s she popularized sporty, casual chic. Her little black dresses and trademark suits were timeless designs that are still popular today. People laughed at the way she dressed, but that was the secret of her success: she didn't look like anyone else. "The most courageous act is to think for yourself. Aloud," she said. Her first success was a dress she fashioned out of an old jersey on a chilly day. Many people asked where she'd bought it. Her response was to offer to make one for them. "My fortune is built on that old jersey that I'd put on because it was cold in Deauville," she said. Chanel's work radiates with her defiance to be completely herself.

Like Chanel, you have to make the most of your uniqueness. No one else can draw from your childhood and teenage experiences, from your school days or from your parents.

Everyone is searching for originality. Ironically, it is right there within them, but most people are too busy being someone else.

Artist Tracey Emin has pulled down the barrier most people keep between their public self and their real self by using her own experiences as subject matter. Her poetic artworks consist of intimate objects most people would not consider showing in public: her unmade, dirty bed with stained sheets; a pack of cigarettes her uncle was holding when he was decapitated in a car crash; and a tent appliquéd with the name of everyone she had ever slept with. She is uncompromisingly herself.

To be successfully creative, you have to realize it's OK to be yourself. Self-knowledge will help you to understand what you have to offer that's special. Ask yourself, "What is the best idea I've ever had?" "How did it come about?" "When am I at my most creative?" Nurture your individual approach and personality. It is more important to be the best version of yourself than a bad copy of someone else.

TO BE NOBODY BUT YOURSELF IN A WORLD
WHICH IS DOING ITS BEST, NIGHT AND DAY, TO
MAKE YOU EVERYBODY ELSE MEANS TO FIGHT
THE HARDEST BATTLE WHICH ANY HUMAN
BEING CAN FIGHT; AND NEVER STOP FIGHTING.

—*e. e. cummings*

More? See why James Joyce benefitted from being self-indulgent on page 109, but why it had the opposite effect on his own daughter on page 119.

be a generator

An actor instinctively disliked auditions because his fate was in others' hands. He realized it was better to create a role rather than wait for a director to give him one. He found an interesting book about a boxer that he thought could be turned into a film, with him playing the lead role. He carried it around with him and showed it to everyone. It was the life story of a boxer called Jake La Motta. He persuaded a film producer to finance a film based on the book. The producer had one condition: that director Martin Scorsese come on board. Scorsese wasn't interested, though—he didn't like boxing and the book wasn't about a significant, champion fighter. This boxer's only talent was absorbing punishment. After months of persuasion, however, Scorsese became intrigued by La Motta's fight with his inner demons and agreed. The film went into production. The actor was Robert De Niro and the film was *Raging Bull*. It was the life story of boxer Jake La Motta. De Niro gained sixty pounds to portray La Motta in his post-boxing years, an extraordinary commitment, and *Raging Bull* went on to become one of the most critically acclaimed films of all time and to win De Niro the Academy Award for Best Actor.

To produce anything of greatness, you have to be proactive and generate it, not sit around and wait. Most people sleepwalk through life, never asking themselves what they're doing, why or if it really matters to them. They absorb the values of their culture, parents and friends, and accept them unquestioningly.

One of my creativity workshop participants was an actor with an interest in Shakespeare. He was attending endless auditions but wasn't getting any roles. We analyzed his predicament. He needed the approval of theater directors to pass the auditions. Why not become your own theater director? I suggested. Put on the play yourself. No money for other actors? Play all the roles yourself. No props? Make them out of cardboard boxes. He became a one-man Shakespeare company. He staged *Hamlet* and played all the parts. His shows were unique, fascinating and unexpected. He became such a huge success he was offered parts in Broadway plays. He turned them down. Why go back to being at the mercy of others' decisions?

The principle applies to everyone. Do you think interdepartmental communication could be better where you work? Then instigate a solution. Do you want to be a writer? Stop sitting waiting for your big idea—just start writing.

We come alive when we're generating something we know is worthwhile. Creative people make their best work happen. If they know that what they're doing is of real significance, they devote all their energy and time to it. Doing what matters is what matters.

> THE LEAST OF THINGS WITH A MEANING IS
> WORTH MORE THAN THE GREATEST OF THINGS
> WITHOUT IT.
>
> — *Carl Jung*

Agree? Discover how Salvador Dalí made things happen on page 98. Disagree? See why money matters just as much as anything else on page 126.

be positive about negatives

Roy Lichtenstein established a reputation as an Abstract Expressionist painter in the 1950s, when that was the dominant style. He produced large, splashy paintings full of dribbles and splatters—standard for the time. His painting was respected and his exhibitions did moderately well. Reviews were reasonable. He swam with the stream.

Suddenly, in 1961, he changed direction. He discarded abstraction and began making large paintings copied from comic-book illustrations. His new work was hard-edged, brash, flat and expressionless, traced from enlarged images. It was the result of a challenge from his young son, who pointed to a Mickey Mouse comic book and said, "I bet you can't paint as good as that, eh, Dad?" So Lichtenstein enlarged and copied one of the illustrations exactly onto canvas.

Lichtenstein's friends hated it. It was their first encounter with Pop Art. They had never seen anything like it. It was the opposite of the emotionally intense Abstract Expressionist paintings they were used to. Comic-book illustrations were worthless, shallow trash in their eyes, symbolizing the worst of American commercialism.

It was the strongest reaction a piece of Lichtenstein's work had ever received. He realized it was better to have a powerful response, even if negative, than the respectful yet muted response he was used to. He produced more comic-book paintings, exhibited them, and the critics savaged them. Again, Lichtenstein reasoned that although it was negative, at least he was achieving a strong reaction. Eventually his iconic Pop Art, comic-book style struck a chord with the younger members of the art world and cemented his place in the history of art.

If others respond strongly to something you've done, that's positive—even if the reaction is negative. What should concern you more than anything is no reaction whatsoever. The history of culture is rife with negativity toward new work and new ideas, to the point where public annoyance can be seen as an endorsement. To be a successful person you often have to create a strong foundation with the bricks others throw at you.

> THE ONLY THING WORSE THAN BEING TALKED
> ABOUT IS NOT BEING TALKED ABOUT.
>
> — *Oscar Wilde*

Convinced? Meet James Dyson, the inventor who just wouldn't give up, on page 53. Not convinced? Meet a pair of guitarists who took advantage of a disadvantage on page 107.

don't think about what others think about

What was it that made one university class so remarkable that every student and the teacher were awarded separate Nobel Prizes?

The astrophysicist Subrahmanyan Chandrasekhar loved his subject. His ideas were so strange that other scientists didn't accept them for years. He worked in relative obscurity. He came up with the model for stellar evolution that became the basis for the theory of black holes. He also was remarkable in another way.

At the University of Chicago, Chandrasekhar was scheduled to teach a class in astrophysics, eighty miles away from the main campus, at the astrological observatory. He was looking forward to it, but only two students signed up. The embarrassingly low attendance was a joke among Chandrasekhar's colleagues. Lecturers pride themselves on popular classes with high attendance. Chandrasekhar was expected to cancel the class because he had to commute the 160 miles along backcountry roads for just two students. But he didn't, because he enjoyed the subject and the classes. He and the two students threw ideas around. They were engrossed in their subject—motivated by the enjoyment of their ideas and fueled by the satisfaction of creating new ways to describe reality. Their fulfillment came from the thrill of reaching new perceptions. It was the smallest class in the history of university education, and was mocked and ridiculed.

A few years later, both of the students won the Nobel Prize in Physics. Later still, Chandrasekhar himself was awarded a Nobel Prize, also for physics. They had the last laugh. It was the most successful university class of all time.

Don't be distracted by the views of others: focus on what engages and inspires you. The most exhilarating experiences are generated in the mind, triggered by information that challenges our thinking. If you're excited by a subject that no one else is, all that should matter to you is that *you're* interested. Revolutionary thinkers who create totally new ideas are driven by their interests, not whether or not others are interested too.

I SWEAR TO GOD, IF I WERE A PIANO PLAYER OR
AN ACTOR OR SOMETHING AND ALL THOSE
DOPES THOUGHT I WAS TERRIFIC, I'D HATE IT. I
WOULDN'T EVEN WANT THEM TO CLAP FOR ME.
PEOPLE ALWAYS CLAP FOR THE WRONG THINGS.

—J. D. Salinger

Disagree? See why others' opinions of you can be worth more than you may think on page 33. Agree? Meet Ed Wood, the zealous filmmaker who was so woefully bad he won awards, on page 85.

doubt everything all the time

Richard Feynman doubted traditional mathematics. That's a pretty big doubt. He created a new math called Feynman diagrams—technically a new kind of algebra, which is now the most widely used in that field. Doubt was central to the thinking of Feynman, a Nobel Prize–winning American, famous for his work on quantum mechanics and particle physics. He doubted everything, constantly, because he realized that if we didn't have doubt, we would not have any new ideas. He believed that nothing was absolutely certain.

Freedom to doubt is the most important aspect of our culture. Doubt should be promoted in every organization and company. Many fear the consequences of doubt, but it is a door to new potential; being unsure gives you the chance to improve the situation. It is absurd to think that we can find out everything there is to know by listening to experts, parents and authorities, without doubting or testing it for ourselves.

It's not just those who seek to revolutionize our understanding of particle physics, like Feynman, who can benefit from doubt. Henry Ford's Model T dominated the car market after he introduced it in 1908. He doubted the lengthy, traditional way in which cars were made and invented the assembly line that enabled cars to be built from the finest materials but cheaply. He doubted the expense of supplying a wide choice of colors; he famously said, "Any customer can have a car painted any color that he wants so long as it is black."

After years of innovations, though, Ford became complacent and stopped doubting. He had no doubt that the Model T was all people needed. By the 1920s, consumers and competitors did start doubting it—why couldn't they have new cars in new colors? Ford nearly destroyed his own company. His son, Edsel, saved the day by doubting his father's strategy, and finally Ford moved with the changing times.

Doubt is a key to unlocking new ideas. Einstein doubted Newton. Picasso doubted Michelangelo. Beethoven doubted Mozart. That's how they moved things forward.

Certainty is a convenient and easy way out of our discomfort. It is the mind's equivalent of fast food—to satisfy our hunger for answers with minimal effort. Doubt, on the other hand, is a great incentive for personal growth. To doubt, to not know, to ask questions, to err and to fail, is the best and only way to learn, grow, progress and create something new.

Doubt what you know. It's important to listen to teachers and experts and seek out knowledge—but at the same time, doubt. Everything that has been achieved over the last five hundred years is because of doubt. Doubt everyone and everything all the time—especially yourself.

DOUBT IS NOT A PLEASANT CONDITION, BUT
CERTAINTY IS ABSURD.

—Voltaire

Still feeling sure of yourself? The next chapter should cure that.

feel inadequate

Do you feel inadequate, that you're not as talented as others? Good. Feeling inadequate is a driving force to do better. The self-satisfied are not the ones producing great things. They're sitting back feeling smug and content.

Over many years of talking to and researching creative people, I've learned that self-doubt is an important motivator. When I was a student at the Royal College of Art, many famous people, such as Ridley Scott, Henry Moore and Dennis Hopper, used to visit to discover the new trends. I was always struck by their humility. I remember the students' surprise when David Bowie, whom all of us were in awe of, was particularly insecure, regarding us as "proper" and "serious" artists and himself as a mere lightweight. The great creative minds are often racked with self-doubt, but they turn it into a driving force, an engine that pushes them forward rather than something that holds them back. Because they feel inadequate, they are driven to prove they are not. They do that by trying to do great things. Self-doubt and passion are a powerful combination.

The greatest artists suffer the greatest self-doubt. Many successful creative people, entrepreneurs, celebrities, artists and writers experience deep feelings of inadequacy—no matter what great successes they achieve.

"Sometimes I wake up in the morning before going off to a shoot, and I think, I can't do this; I'm a fraud. They're going to fire me—all these things. I'm fat; I'm ugly . . ." admitted the actress Kate Winslet, despite being the youngest person ever to acquire six Academy Award nominations and winning Best Actress for *The Reader*. Self-doubt and high standards are a powerful combination.

Although he exuded self-confidence, John Lennon was

surprisingly insecure and suffered from a deep lack of self-esteem. Lennon wrote the lyrics of the song "Help!" to express his confusion after the Beatles' meteoric rise to success: "I was fat and depressed and I was crying out for help." It was the first chink in the armor of Lennon's self-protection. All his life, even when Beatlemania peaked, despite more number one singles and albums than any other group and breaking world records for concert attendance and television viewings, he still had poor self-esteem. It was the key force that drove him to do better and better.

Many successful creative people secretly worry that others will find out that they're not clever and capable. They expect the no-talent police to come and arrest them at any moment. They take little credit for their successes and attribute them to luck. But that is why they strive so hard. Self-doubt keeps them diligent. Fear of failure is a great motivator and it keeps the creative ego in check.

I DON'T BELIEVE ANYONE EVER SUSPECTS HOW COMPLETELY UNSURE I AM OF MY WORK AND MYSELF AND WHAT TORTURES OF SELF-DOUBTING THE DOUBT OF OTHERS HAS ALWAYS GIVEN ME.

—*Tennessee Williams*

More? If you liked doubt, you'll love ignorance, on page 95. Less? If you've had enough of self-doubt for now, try page 61.

be practically useless

The Juicy Salif is a lemon squeezer that doesn't work. Yet it's also a design icon and a huge commercial success. Why?

The design consists of a teardrop body supported by three legs, cast from aluminum, a metal that we associate with modernity and aircraft. What makes the squeezer so distinctive and therefore so popular is that it is imbued with the personality of its creator, Philippe Starck. It brings together all of his obsessions. It's been exhibited in the Museum of Modern Art, so it's not just design, but art.

Starck designed the Juicy Salif in a restaurant while eating squid. He squeezed lemon over the squid, wondered if the shape of the squid could be used as the basis for a lemon squeezer and started sketching on a napkin (now on permanent display in Milan's Alessi Museum).

As a child, Starck was fascinated by science-fiction comics and spent hours redrawing spaceships. His father was an aircraft designer, and Starck was enthralled by the sleek lines of the aluminum craft. Another of his passions was the diverse shapes of animals and plants. The result of these disparate influences, the lemon squeezer was successful *because* it was personal. He didn't ask chefs and cooks to test prototypes and adapt it to their needs. He made it the way he wanted to.

One of the key ingredients of the success of the Juicy Salif was that it didn't work. Its height made it unstable, lemon juice dribbled down the legs, and its feet scratched kitchen work surfaces. You might expect this to detract from its reputation, but no, it enhanced it. The public identified with the view that expression was more important than function and that it's the idea that counts. The fact that it was dysfunctional became its unique selling point.

The genuinely innovative are led by their passions and not by rational ambitions. New ideas spring from personal interests, even if they seem irrelevant to the task at hand. Innovative people put practical considerations aside because thinking about logistics leads to thinking logically, which ties down the leaps of the mind required to create something unique.

Another design icon that breaks the rules of practicality is the "Well Tempered Chair," produced by Ron Arad. It makes the sitter ill-tempered because it's made from sheets of steel and is too uncomfortable to sit on. The infamous fashion designer Alexander McQueen designed shoes that were impossible to walk in and clothes that couldn't be worn. Architects Renzo Piano and Richard Rogers designed the Pompidou Centre in Paris inside out. Utilitarian features such as escalators, plumbing, air vents and electrical cables were put on the outside, freeing up space inside for exhibitions and events. The futuristic design led to spiralling maintenance costs because it required constant repainting.

All these creative thinkers poured their obsessions into their work and ignored the rule that "form follows function."

To be true to an idea, you have to value expression over perfection, vitality over finish, movement over the static, expression over perfection and form over function. Put your personality before practicality and your individuality into everything.

> IT'S THE ADDICTS THAT STAY WITH IT.
> THEY'RE NOT NECESSARILY THE MOST
> TALENTED, THEY'RE JUST THE ONES THAT
> CAN'T GET IT OUT OF THEIR SYSTEMS.
>
> —*Harold Brown*

Now meet the most famous example of imperfection in the world on page 51.

be perceptive about perception

The great nineteenth-century engineer Isambard Kingdom Brunel is remembered for railways, bridges and the first propeller-driven steamships. Yet his most innovative construction was his image. The famous photograph of Brunel standing before the launching chains of the SS *Great Eastern* created an idea of Brunel as a romantic genius, arrogantly relaxed and confident. Although it looks like a snapshot of an insouciant savant taking a break, it was actually a painstaking act of image manipulation.

This classic "snapshot" in fact took several days to construct. In the other photos taken on the shoot, although artfully posed, Brunel appears hesitant, insignificant, balding, conservative and inconsequential against the backdrop of huge chains and ships. Yet one photo struck the right note.

Both the photographer and Brunel were searching for an *idealized* image. In the 1850s, taking photos outdoors was arduous and extremely time-consuming. It required a huge amount of equipment, including a portable darkroom with an arsenal of toxic chemicals. Brunel had many demanding projects requiring his time at this point, but he ignored them all because he appreciated the importance of the photograph. Brunel understood the effect the photo would have on public awareness of him and therefore his work.

The photographer took many photos over several days, and eventually they hit on the magic image that is cemented in the public's imagination. The photographer understood that the purpose of the photograph is not to reproduce reality but to create a new reality of the same intensity.

Brunel arguably owes his legacy and place in history to that photographer more than he does his engineering works.

Be aware of how your audience perceives and understands things, and appreciate that the aura created around a person, place, and work affects how people respond to them. To get audiences to take your work seriously, it's necessary to get them to take *you* seriously.

WE CAN CONTROL OUR LIVES BY CONTROLLING
OUR PERCEPTIONS.

—*Bruce Lipton*

ART IS NOT SUPPOSED TO CHANGE THE WORLD,
TO CHANGE PRACTICAL THINGS, BUT TO
CHANGE PERCEPTIONS. ART CAN CHANGE THE
WAY WE SEE THE WORLD.

—*JR*

Not interested in improving your own image? Consider becoming anonymous on page 145 or discover the benefits of being as annoying as possible on page 174.

be naturally inspired

The structural strength and beauty of the bird's nest is remarkable, but how could it be used on a human scale? Architects

Herzog and De Meuron responded to this question by producing one of the most spectacular buildings of recent times, the "Bird's Nest" Stadium, to be the centerpiece of the 2008 Beijing Olympics. The façade consists of thousands of steel "twigs," infilled with translucent panels that have the insulating qualities of mud, feathers and moss in a real bird's nest. The panels protect spectators from wind and rain but cleverly allow sunlight to seep through to feed the grass.

The stadium achieved its aspiration to be a global landmark. The intoxicating beauty of the elliptical latticework shell is an aesthetic triumph that cemented China's reputation as the place for courageous creative risk-taking. Even more impressive is that the radical structure tore up the rules of modernism that had become a kind of authoritarianism.

Whatever field you work in, nature can always provide you with new insights. Nature is creative by necessity. It is the consummate problem-solver. Animals, plants and microbes are skilled inventors and the ultimate engineers. After 3.8 billion years of evolution, they have found what works and, most importantly, what lasts. Creative thinkers don't think in terms of what they can copy from the natural world, but what they can learn from it. They study nature's best ideas and then imitate them to solve diverse problems.

Nike designers observed mountain goats at the Oregon Zoo and developed Goatek Traction, an all-terrain shoe. While traveling in Canada, Clarence Birdseye ate some fish that had been naturally frozen and later thawed. He borrowed nature's idea, and the frozen-food industry took off. A doctor recalled signaling to childhood friends by knocking on a hollow log; from this observation he invented the stethoscope. J. M. W. Turner strapped himself to the mast of a ship in a vicious storm to observe nature and capture its essence in his paintings. Jørn Utzon's iconic design for the Sydney Opera House was inspired by a cut-up orange he had for lunch: the fourteen shells of the building, if assembled together, would form a perfect sphere. George de Mestral, when walking in the country, noticed how burrs stuck to his clothing. By mimicking the small hooks of the burrs he developed Velcro. Japan's Shinkansen bullet train is modeled on the kingfisher's aerodynamic beak. Intertwining ivies that hung in the form of a catenary arch inspired the design of the suspension bridge. Many composers have used birdsong for inspiration: Olivier Messiaen was a particular exponent, and so too were Beethoven, Handel, Mahler and Delius.

Many Silicon Valley companies modeled the way they organize their corporations on living organisms. This enables them to adapt rapidly to changes and restructure themselves quickly in response to market developments.

Whatever your field, nature has produced something that relates to your subject. Explore the animal, vegetable and mineral kingdoms. What can they teach you? Think of nature not as a source of materials to use but as a library of ideas.

THERE IS NO BETTER DESIGNER THAN NATURE.

—Alexander McQueen

Keen for natural inspiration but not interested in being practical? Try page 30. Curious about transcending natural limits? Consider trying a twenty-six-hour body clock on page 93.

don't be an expert on yourself

If you give a lecture or talk about yourself or your work, try to embrace the following attitude: *I'm not sure what I do or why; let's work it out together.* I once attended a talk by a speaker who spent the first twenty-five minutes telling us how important he was and that he was an expert in his field. It was counterproductive. We all sat there thinking, if you have to tell us how important you are, you're not very important. By chance, soon after that I attended a talk by a famous sculptor who completely disarmed the audience by opening with the assertion that he didn't really understand his work: he tried things out and people seemed to think it was successful so he kept doing it. He asked us, the audience, to explain his work for him. You will only get the most out of your talk if it teaches you about yourself.

(I once chose to give a lecture from a parking lot. I drew images on large sheets of paper with a thick pen and shouted up to my audience, who were leaning out of the second-floor windows. They were uncomfortable. I was uncomfortable. That was the point. It forced me to reduce everything to the essentials.)

Another time, I gave a talk in a lecture theater full of entrepreneurs and businessmen. My theme was that we are all too easily distracted and need to be more alert and focused. I hired twenty nude male and female models to walk among the audience as I spoke. I assumed the audience would all be distracted. I had underestimated them—they were intelligent, focused individuals and listened attentively to each word, as I discovered at the question-and-answer session at the end. It didn't matter. The lecture was unforgettable.

If you want to engage an audience, it's essential to be engaged yourself. Only give a talk about something you care passionately about. As part of my work at universities I've had to listen to talks on subjects I have no interest in, but if the speaker is passionately interested, I find that I too become absorbed.

THE ATTRACTION OF THE VIRTUOSO FOR THE
PUBLIC IS VERY LIKE THAT OF THE CIRCUS FOR
THE CROWD. THERE IS ALWAYS THE HOPE THAT
SOMETHING DANGEROUS WILL HAPPEN.

— Claude Debussy

Agree? Rail further against the tyranny of experts on page 26.
Disagree? See why nudity only really aids public speaking when
taken to extremes on page 38.

be stubborn about compromise

A teenager passionately wanted to become a writer, but his parents
considered this madness. They wanted him to become a lawyer, a
secure, respectable profession. To "save" him from his writing
ambitions, his parents had him committed three times to a mental institution, where he was subjected to electroshock therapy. He
refused to compromise. He instinctively knew he was meant to be
a writer, and he went on to become an author with a unique vision.
The incredible struggle of Paulo Coelho is an extraordinary example of sheer determination. His book *The Alchemist* was translated
into sixty languages, sold forty million copies worldwide and
provided Coelho with unequivocal, lasting financial security.

Creative thinkers appreciate that to compromise and take the sensible and safe route would be a disaster. When Todd McFarlane worked as an illustrator for Marvel Comics, executives told him to tone down his work because it was too gruesome for the Marvel readership. McFarlane quit. He gave up the security of a steady career and started his own company. His hugely successful ventures span publishing, toy production and a film and animation studio. As an artist in business, McFarlane has remained true to his artistic vision, no matter what the business cost.

We all come under pressure from our employers, family or friends to compromise, but to make something unique, to do something extraordinary, often requires that you refuse to compromise your ideals. You have no responsibility to live up to others' expectations, but you do have a responsibility to live up to your own.

YOUR TIME IS LIMITED; SO DON'T WASTE IT LIVING SOMEONE ELSE'S LIFE. DON'T BE TRAPPED BY DOGMA—WHICH IS LIVING WITH THE RESULTS OF OTHER PEOPLE'S THINKING. DON'T LET THE NOISE OF OTHERS' OPINIONS DROWN OUT YOUR OWN INNER VOICE.

— *Steve Jobs*

Meet some other writers who refused to give up on page 172.

be a weapon of mass creation

We owe a great deal to economist Paul Samuelson. In 2008, when the international economy slid into the steepest downturn since the Great Depression, industrialized countries averted disaster by following Samuelson's counterintuitive advice and raising spending on infrastructure projects, cutting taxes, allowing imports to flow in and driving interest rates down to near zero. Contrast this with the Great Depression of the 1930s, when governments turned a crisis into a disaster by cutting spending, balancing budgets and erecting trade barriers.

When John F. Kennedy was elected in 1960, he appointed Samuelson as his economic adviser, but then was shocked by his recommendation. The economy was facing a downturn, and Samuelson told Kennedy to cut taxes. It was counterintuitive and seemed to be the opposite policy to Kennedy's election campaign promise to balance the budget. After Kennedy's assassination, Lyndon B. Johnson carried out the plan and the economy bounced back. Samuelson remained adviser to subsequent presidents.

Even more shocking was that many of Samuelson's economic theories were inspired by concepts from medicine and physics. For decades he read medical journals in search of ideas that could be transferred to economics, such as Mendelian dynamics. He also applied the equilibrium principles of thermodynamics to economics. He had such a huge impact because he applied creative thinking to economics when everyone else was applying logic.

When he was a student in the 1930s, Samuelson attended a lecture on economics at the University of Chicago. It was a revelation to him; he realized there and then that he wanted to be an economist. What he brought to the stodgy world of currency graphs, growth estimates and supply-and-demand debates was a creative mind. Discovering his calling made him more alive, more vibrant and more authentic—and this playfulness and inventiveness is what made him so distinguished. He had fun with ideas rather than trying to write Very Serious Papers. His books were at times so playful they toppled over into inspired childishness. In a footnote to his influential paper "Overlapping Generations Model," he wrote, "Surely, no sentence beginning with the word 'surely' can validly contain a question mark at its end? However, one paradox is enough for one article . . ."

Samuelson felt that economics was made for him, and that he was made for it. "Always, I have been overpaid to do what has been pure fun," he said.

Economics was not known for being a creative endeavor; it was a discipline dominated by stale, stuffy and repetitious thinking. Samuelson changed all that. Applying creative thinking in an "uncreative" field gives you an advantage. Like the one-eyed man in the kingdom of the blind, if you think creatively where no one else is, it gives you the edge.

> IF YOU DELIBERATELY PLAN ON BEING LESS
> THAN YOU ARE CAPABLE OF BEING, THEN I
> WARN YOU THAT YOU'LL BE DEEPLY UNHAPPY
> FOR THE REST OF YOUR LIFE. YOU WILL BE
> EVADING YOUR OWN CAPACITIES, YOUR OWN
> POSSIBILITIES.
>
> —*Abraham Maslow*

Meet a great inventor who found creativity where he least expected it on page 55.

get into what you're into

An agency was struggling to come up with ideas for a TV ad and asked for my help. The target audience was the elderly. The ad agency had extensively researched every aspect of the lives of the elderly, but it meant little to the two young men working on the ad. They were outside their subject looking in.

I made them *be* their subject. I took them both to a theatrical costumer and had them dressed in gray wigs and prosthetic teeth. Their faces were aged with latex molds, and they were given walking sticks and appropriate clothes. They were transformed into authentic-looking eighty-year-olds. The transformation was quite shocking.

I simply asked them to walk around the streets and shops of London. They were astonished by the change in attitude toward them. At best, people were patronizing; more often, they were dismissive or rude. It was a harrowing experience. Suddenly they understood how it felt to be elderly. This experience formed the idea for their ad.

We tend to stand outside what we do, looking in. Detached and analytical. To get the most out of life and work, we need to see it from the inside. Whatever you are interested in, get right into it. Imagine you are the subject of your project. If your subject is a cup, try to imagine what it is like to be a cup, to be picked up, to have boiling water poured into you, to smell like coffee, to be put in a dishwasher, to be scratched or chipped. Be the subject from the inside out.

ONE HAD TO IMMERSE ONESELF IN ONE'S
SURROUNDINGS AND INTENSELY STUDY
NATURE OR ONE'S SUBJECT TO UNDERSTAND
HOW TO RECREATE IT.

— *Paul Cézanne*

Seeking a new perspective? Teach someone a lesson on page 188.

Cut it out

The epic war film *Apocalypse Now* is consistently voted one of the greatest films of all time. Filming started in March 1976 and was scheduled to take six weeks. It took sixteen months. The director, Francis Ford Coppola, shot around 230 hours of footage, with multiple takes of the same scene. He was hoping to capture a magical or unusual performance. He encouraged the actors to ad-lib, which produced some poetic moments but also hours of unusable footage. Once filming was finished, the movie had to be cut and recut for months. It took Coppola and his film editor Walter Murch nearly three years to edit the footage into the finished *Apocalypse Now*.

Why produce a lot of work and then throw away 95 percent? The two processes seem contradictory. Why not just produce the 5 percent ultimately used? Because you don't know *which* 5 percent that will be. Editing can be hard because you're discarding things you have put a lot of energy into making. Yet often what we see of creative thinkers' work is the tip of the iceberg. We don't see the hours, days, weeks and months of hard work and struggle; we just see the end result.

Picasso would have empathized with Coppola. A friend of mine is a specialist picture restorer who conserves paintings by Rembrandt, Titian, Matisse and many other great artists for major museums of the world. For one job, he was flown to Paris twice a year with his team of assistants and taken down into a vast subterranean vault beneath a bank. The armored, bomb-proof walls were a meter thick. The two-meter-thick vault doors could only be accessed by an elaborate system of voice recognition and three-foot keys. It required two bank staff to cooperate and open the complex lock simultaneously. Then there were body heat detectors, Doppler radar, magnetic fields and motion detectors. Finally they would emerge into a vast temperature-controlled vault that stretched as far as the eye could see. It was lined on either side by racks containing tens of thousands of unseen Picasso paintings. My friend's task was to inspect them for aging and make any necessary repairs or restoration. Although Picasso had produced thousands of paintings over his lifetime, he only ever selected the best 5 percent for exhibition. The rest remained in the vault.

If you produce one hundred ideas, one of them is likely to be great. If you produce five ideas, the chances of one being great are small. When a company calls me in to work as a creative consultant on a project, instead of getting them to come up with one idea, I get them to come up with a hundred. The first forty ideas are obvious. The next forty are unusual and offbeat. The last twenty are strange and surreal because the participants are pushing their minds into areas they've never been before. It is usually one of the ideas from the last twenty that we use. Ninety-nine are cut out. Challenge yourself to generate more ideas, and more work, with less attachment. When it's time to make tough choices, you'll know you're sharing your best work.

KILL YOUR DARLINGS, KILL YOUR DARLINGS, EVEN
WHEN IT BREAKS YOUR EGOCENTRIC LITTLE
SCRIBBLER'S HEART, KILL YOUR DARLINGS.

—*Stephen King*

Can't bring yourself to cut your creative efforts? Try reworking them instead, on page 143.

grow up without growing old

When artist Georgia O'Keeffe was eighty-four, she shocked her neighbors in the small town of Abiquiú, New Mexico, with her method for rejuvenating herself.

She understood that it takes years to build up the ability to understand yourself, the world you live in and your field of expertise—and crucially maintain a fresh, childlike attitude. The architect Zaha Hadid didn't achieve international respect and win awards for her unique designs until she was over fifty.

Paul Cézanne had his first one-man show at the age of fifty-six. Alfred Hitchcock didn't fully develop his trademark sense of suspense in his films until after he had turned fifty. Jane Austen published her first novel after she was thirty-five. Joseph Conrad's work was first published when he was thirty-seven. Charles Darwin was fifty years old when he proposed the theory of evolution in *On the Origin of Species*—which sold out on its first day of release.

Georgia O'Keeffe produced remarkable images of the American landscape and still lifes, painted with intimacy and stark precision. O'Keeffe was already in her fifties when she started to gain significant attention, and throughout her sixties and seventies her fame grew gradually. Her most important exhibition, at the Whitney Museum of American Art, did not come until 1970, when she was in her eighties. It established her as one of America's most significant painters. She didn't grow old in mind because her enthusiasm never waned. At the age of eighty-four, when she was famous, O'Keeffe was rejuvenated by a twenty-six-year-old potter, Juan Hamilton. The two scandalized their neighbors in Abiquiú with their liaison. They ignored their notoriety, traveled the world together and invigorated each other. They were together until O'Keeffe died at the age of ninety-eight.

It takes years to build up the ability to understand yourself, the world you live in and your field of expertise.

Many entrepreneurs, chefs, teachers, writers and artists produce their greatest work as their insights and perceptions deepen with age. Maturity is an advantage when it comes to creativity. The more experience of life you have had, the more subject matter there is to draw on. Age brings an understanding of who you are and what your limits are. Creativity is about having something to say.

Creative people can't refuse to grow old, but they can refuse to grow up. They maintain the playful attitude of a child throughout their lives. They understand that some things are too serious to take seriously. They never lose the urge to throw a snowball at a sacred cow. All creativity is about mind over matter. That matter might be paint, ink, paper or almost anything. The matter doesn't matter, because it's all in the mind.

MY BREAKTHROUGH CAME VERY LATE IN LIFE, REALLY ONLY STARTING WHEN I WAS FIFTY YEARS OLD. BUT AT THAT TIME I FELT AS THOUGH I HAD THE STRENGTH FOR NEW DEEDS AND IDEAS.

—Edvard Munch

Inspired? Be mature enough to be childish on page 72.

If it ain't broke, break it

I have been obsessed with a woman in the reception area of Central Saint Martins College of Art where I work, for years. I look for her every week as I pass by. My fascination with her never dims. She doesn't exist in our world but in a mysterious and ethereal zone. Her delicate flesh has been exquisitely modeled. Serene and remote, her head is turned slightly away as I pass. With an air of aloofness, her gaze has never met mine. She lost both arms in an accident, but that simply adds to her enigma.

She's a plaster cast of the original *Venus de Milo*. To catch a glimpse of her in the Louvre you have to elbow your way through crowds. Further proof of her enduring popularity is the way she's plastered over mugs, underpants and coasters and reproduced as soap, saltshakers and rubber toys that squeak. She has also inspired artists such as Cézanne, Dalí and Magritte. When the statue was sent to Japan on loan in 1964, one and a half million people were carried past her on a moving sidewalk.

The *Venus de Milo* is full of faults, yet she is the quintessential emblem of classical beauty. The graceful statue of a mysterious, nameless goddess has intrigued and fascinated the world since its discovery in 1820, when it achieved instant fame. It's a classical sculpture that follows an unusually dynamic spiral composition.

Many ancient statues of Venus exist, but most are too damaged to compete with the *Venus de Milo*, and the remainder are not damaged enough. The statue would have been painted and adorned with jewelry to look lifelike. All traces of original paint have disappeared, and the only signs of the armbands, necklace, earrings and crown she used to wear are the attachment holes. Famously, the arms have also been lost. Broken and mutilated she stands; no one knows her original pose. She may have held an apple, a crown, a shield or a mirror in which she admired her reflection. We'll never know. It all adds to her intrigue and allure. This is the beauty of imperfection. It is more enlightened to appreciate imperfections; if you search for perfection you will always be disappointed. There is a sense of freedom in accepting its alternative.

The coffee chain Starbucks embraced imperfection. They introduced new concepts quickly. Whether an iced caramel macchiato or a new store design, these concepts were launched before they had been perfected and then improved as they went along. An innovation process that is trying to achieve something faultless is too slow and restricted. Innovation requires errors and failures because they lead to new ideas. The conundrum for organizations is how to foster an innovative culture, with all the messiness and faults that come with it, when the perfectionists in an organization work to reject imperfection.

Perfectionism can be a roadblock to new ideas; it is a full stop, whereas imperfection can lead somewhere unexpected. High standards are worthwhile, but perfectionism is another story.

When my daughter, Scarlet, was at school, she had to produce a self-portrait for an art exam. She felt uncomfortable about it, so she portrayed herself through frosted glass. It obscured the detail of her features but created a mysterious, blurred and intriguing image. She was worried about the response to a self-portrait that didn't clearly show her face. Her teachers loved it and so too did London's Saatchi Gallery, which later included it in an exhibition.

Strive for imperfection. Miss deadlines, get lost on the way to the airport, forget to reply to emails and show up at parties a day early. It's more interesting. If it's broke, don't fix it; if it ain't broke, break it.

THE ESSENCE OF BEING HUMAN IS THAT ONE
DOES NOT SEEK PERFECTION.

— *George Orwell*

Agree? Plan to have more accidents on page 82. Disagree? Discover the merits of perseverance and perfectionism through one of history's great inventors in the next chapter.

Pick yourself up

A Central Saint Martins alumnus became frustrated with his Hoover when vacuuming at home. The dust bag kept clogging with dust and reducing suction. He thought of the powerful air filter in the spray-paint room in the factory where he worked. "If only I could put that filter in the Hoover," he thought. So he tried. He worked for the next five years, designing, making and testing more than 5,000 prototypes. That means 4,999 failures that he had to pick himself up from. Quite a task. He also had to finance it all himself.

When he finally produced a satisfactory model, he tried to sell it to manufacturers of traditional bag-type vacuum cleaners, but they all rejected his bagless device. Eventually he sold his vacuum cleaner through catalogue sales in Japan, where it became a commercial success and won a design prize. His problems didn't end there, though. He still failed to sell his idea to a major manufacturer and had to open his own manufacturing company. No easy feat. The designer was James Dyson, and within two years his Dual Cyclone model became the top-selling vacuum cleaner in Britain and spread across the world. Dyson's elegant and practical appliances have gone on to win many design awards and to be exhibited in art and design museums around the world.

I meet a great many talented artists, writers and musicians

in my work as a lecturer, both at Central Saint Martins and in the art world. Many go on to be successful, but many others don't. What distinguishes the successful from the unsuccessful is the way they deal with the inevitable disappointments and difficulties that arise. Psychologists call it the 90-10 principle. Ten percent of life is what happens to you, and 90 percent is decided by how you react to it. We have no control over what happens to us—high winds rip the roof off, your train is delayed, or a meteorite lands on your car. The 90 percent, however, is up to you.

What sets successful creative people apart is their reaction to negative events. Some people fall into a downward spiral of negativity and abandon their project. The creative thinker is able to put aside his or her annoyance and adopt a positive attitude—and therefore achieve a positive result. I was waiting for a train with my son Louis once when the station loudspeakers announced that it had been delayed by an hour. The other passengers started moaning and angrily shouting at the railway staff. For them the next hour was dead time. For Louis it was an opportunity. He took out his sketchpad and started drawing the angry passengers. He was disappointed when the train arrived. His reaction was a reminder to me that there is no "dead time": we can always be doing something like writing, drawing or just observing.

Creative thinkers channel their negative feelings into something useful. Everyone is irritable and disappointed when things go wrong, but creative thinkers quickly rally and try again.

Their desire to produce something excellent overrides momentary failure. Attitude is more important than ability.

> THE PEOPLE WHO ARE CRAZY ENOUGH TO
> THINK THEY CAN CHANGE THE WORLD, ARE
> THE ONES WHO DO.
>
> —*Apple's 1997 "Think Different" commercial*

Meet Ted Turner, the entrepreneur who truly made things happen, on page 158.

Challenge the challenging

When the great inventor Thomas Edison hired bright young engineer Nikola Tesla to work in his New York office in 1884, he took on more than he had bargained for. Tesla had been recommended because he was considered to be a genius comparable to Edison. Tesla designed several products for Edison, but didn't receive his promised bonus ($1 million in today's money), so he stormed out.

Edison's use of direct current (DC) to carry electricity to consumers was a monopoly. Tesla invented a new method using alternating current (AC). Unlike DC, it could transmit huge amounts of power over long distances. Edison condemned Tesla's AC as dangerous because of its high voltage, and he demonstrated this by publicly electrocuting an elephant in New York in August 1890. The botched and horrific killing needed two attempts. It didn't stop an investor from backing Tesla's AC technology, and eventually Tesla won through. The bitter rivalry bore fruit.

Having a rival can be useful, as rivals drive us to the limits of our ability. Edison went head-to-head with Tesla, Bill Gates with Steve Jobs, and for Constable there was Turner. They all benefitted from their rivalry, pushing each other to greater things. In hard times, when they struggled for motivation, each was spurred on by the achievements of the other. Competition can help everyone reach greater heights. It creates intensity and passion and makes you work harder and better. If there is someone in your office, factory or workplace who constantly tries to outdo you, rise to the challenge.

During the 1920s, brothers Adolf and Rudolf created the Dassler Brothers Sports Shoe Company, a business based in their mother's laundry room in Herzogenaurach, Germany. By 1948 they had split the company into separate firms, with each of them running one of two competing factories on opposite sides of town. Their equal determination to produce the better sneaker led them to be world leaders in their field: Adolf's company was Adidas, and Rudolf's was Puma. Herzogenaurach became known as "the town of bent necks" because residents were constantly checking to see which of the two brands their neighbors were wearing.

As with the Dasslers, it helps if your competitor is roughly at the same level as you, not a great deal lower or higher, because then you have a realistic chance of outdoing your rival. In 2012 Apple was declared the biggest company in the world. Steve Jobs hadn't set out to overtake the biggest companies of the time, Coke or Nike, though; his rivalry was with Bill Gates. They were the same age, had started their businesses at the same time and in similarly humble circumstances and were on an equal level of success. The fruits of their rivalry were Microsoft's Windows, which became the world's default operating system, and Apple's iPhone, iPad and iPod. "And every fantasy we had about creating products and learning new things—we achieved all of it. And most of it as rivals," said Bill Gates. In 1997 Apple was facing financial doom. Their unlikely savior? Microsoft, who stepped in to save them by investing $150 million in Apple shares. Why did Gates bail out Apple? Perhaps he sensed that he needed Jobs's rivalry. They had a mutual respect and became friendly in the years before Jobs died. Having fought each other for so long, each knew better than anyone what the other had accomplished.

Psychology tells us that rivalry has the potential to both help and hinder creative success—it all depends on how we handle the competition. The benefits of competitiveness were demonstrated by psychologists in a study led by Tim Rees at the University of Exeter. They recruited students to carry out a darts challenge while blindfolded, and a researcher dressed as a supporter of a rival university tried to demoralize the students by criticizing their performance. The students' later performances were better because they were motivated to prove their rival wrong.

Whatever your field, embrace competition: it can make you strive to be better, to go that extra mile. Chances are, you too have at least one close rival. Monitor that rival's achievements with admiration, and a touch of envy. Then get back to work.

I'M NOT GOING TO GET INTO THE RING WITH TOLSTOY.

— *Ernest Hemingway*

Feeling collaborative rather than competitive? Meet the scientist without whom you probably wouldn't be alive on page 164.

find out how to find out

I vividly remember walking along Fifth Avenue in New York on my first trip there, passing block after block of rectangular, ornamented apartment houses, oppressive in their uniformity, monotonous in their regularity. Then the gleaming white Solomon R. Guggenheim Museum burst into view, a breathtaking symphony of ovals, arcs and circles.

This museum doesn't look like any building you've ever seen before. That's because the architect, Frank Lloyd Wright, was self-taught. He had to work out for himself how to design a building. Wright found his own way. Ignorance of the "right" way to do something can be an asset; if you do things the way they've been taught, your methods will be the same as everyone else's and you'll produce something obvious, predictable. Lack of knowledge can provide fresh perspectives.

The Guggenheim is as impressive inside as out. A spiral ramp rises through the building to a domed skylight. It is a unique concept that delights visitors and provides an original way of displaying contemporary art. The circle is the form that echoes through the building, from the rotunda to the terrazzo floors. By discarding the static box shapes of conventional museums, Wright produced a building that's as refreshing now as it was when it first opened in 1959. Every major museum is indebted to the Guggenheim; it has made it acceptable for an architect to design an expressive, intensely personal museum.

Frank Lloyd Wright attended Madison High School in Wisconsin, but didn't graduate. He was admitted to university but left without taking a degree. He was hired as a draftsman for an architectural firm and taught himself about architecture. He designed many houses with the radical approach of using the mass-produced materials developed for commercial buildings. Wright rejected the elaborate compartmentalization of the time and created bold, plain walls, roomy family living spaces and large glazed areas. His technical deficiencies meant that he often overlooked mundane practicalities, and so his roofs leaked, he ignored budgets, and his buildings were beset by a host of technical problems; but his clients appreciated that they were getting a design classic.

Wright consistently broke the rules. Not to be rebellious— he simply hadn't been taught them. He produced work that felt right to him. Sometimes, knowing the "right way" can be a disadvantage.

We don't learn to walk by reading a book on how to walk. We learn by walking, falling over, getting up and trying again. There is no right way of doing anything. You must find your way. Wherever you work, try to discover for yourself how to do things. You just might find a new and better way.

IF I'D OBSERVED ALL THE RULES, I'D NEVER HAVE GOT ANYWHERE.

—*Marilyn Monroe*

Discover the joys of doubting everyone and everything on page 25.

leave an impression

The names of ex-students killed in World War II were carved on a plaque at Yale University. A sculpture student, Maya Lin, couldn't resist running her fingers over them whenever she passed by. Touching the grooves of the names gave her a sense of deep connection with the fallen soldiers. It was something she never forgot.

Lin remembered that sensation when designing the groundbreaking Vietnam Veterans Memorial in Washington, DC, a long, black stone wall with the names of all fallen soldiers carved on it. There are no ranks or details; everyone is equal. There are sixty thousand names. The stone was chosen for its reflective quality; when visitors look at the wall, their reflection can be seen simultaneously with the engraved names, symbolically bringing the past and present together. Most memorials are remote and untouchable bronze sculptures of soldiers, but over the decades millions of visitors have run their fingers across the carved names of the Vietnam Memorial. Even if you don't know anyone who died in Vietnam, it's heartrending to watch visitors earnestly studying the names to find their loved ones, or rubbing pencil on paper held against a name etched into the wall.

Creativity can be as simple as pointing out something

incredible that everyone else hasn't noticed. Note anything that astounds you, no matter how small. You never know when you might be able to use it. If it left an impression on you, it will leave an impression on others.

ART IS NOT WHAT YOU SEE, BUT WHAT YOU
MAKE OTHERS SEE.

—Edgar Degas

Inspired? Join Truman Capote in refusing to overlook the overlooked on page 96. Uninspired? Forget about making an impression on others and meet the most successful class in history, in which every student won a Nobel Prize, on page 23.

design a difference

A package arrived and I tore it open expectantly. Inside was something unexpected. A sleek, fourteen-inch, egg-shaped object. The white-and-turquoise shell was translucent like polished ice but tougher than bulletproof glass. The color combination was new and oddly alien. The egg's vitreous nature allowed me a blurry glimpse of the innards. The smoothness, absence of joints or grooves and magical weightlessness made it feel as though it could not have been created in a factory but only by alchemy. It seemed like an object from another universe, a visual wonder that you needed to run your hands over to believe it was real. It was otherworldly, created by an alien culture far more technologically advanced than any previously encountered.

Luckily the object had a plug that fit into our earthly sockets. I powered it up and an apple appeared on its screen. I had been sent the new iMac G3. Back in the late 1990s, it seemed unearthly. Like a lot of other people, I began to wonder what magician had created it and what supernatural powers he'd used.

Steve Jobs used his small amount of knowledge about design to make a big difference. Apple products became famous for style. While their competitors concentrated on the technical aspects of computers, Jobs focused on aesthetics. Until the iMac, computers had been ugly and uncool. What made Jobs think so differently?

In college, he had attended only the classes he liked, the ones that interested him. He saw a beautifully designed poster advertising a calligraphy class. It was so appealing that he felt compelled to attend. He learned about the design of typefaces, each with its own unique personality, and the importance of the appearance of lettering. There was as much meaning conveyed by the design of a typeface as the words it was used to express. Typography was functional, but could also be beautiful and seductive. Jobs found it artistically subtle in a way science couldn't capture. This small piece of knowledge turned out to be hugely significant, for all of us.

Jobs positioned Apple at the intersection of art and computing; he united technology and design, and introduced elegance and style to a product that up until then had been geeky and clumsy. Inspired by that typography course, the Mac had numerous typefaces and an emphasis on design. This gave Apple the edge over its rivals. Windows copied Jobs's values; in this way, all personal computers were influenced. Apple was not a technological innovator; it remade other company's ideas. IBM introduced the personal computer first; Nokia invented the smartphone first. When Apple tried innovation it was hopeless. Remember the Newton? The Power Mac G4 Cube? Neither does anyone else. "We did tablets, lots of tablets, well before Apple did. But they put the pieces together in a way that succeeded," recalled Bill Gates. As Jobs observed, "For you to sleep well at night, the aesthetic, the quality, has to be carried all the way through."

Entrepreneurs and creative thinkers make the most of whatever information they have, however little. Armed with a small amount of knowledge, Jobs fought against the conventional thinking of the computer industry and won. A small nugget of knowledge that you've overlooked could be the key that unlocks doors that have previously been closed.

THE DIFFERENCE BETWEEN ORDINARY AND
EXTRAORDINARY IS THAT LITTLE EXTRA.

—Jimmy Johnson

Meet the world's best designed—and least functional—kitchen implement on page 30.

be as incompetent as possible

I sat and watched a clock for twenty-four hours, completely enthralled.

Artist Christian Marclay's film installation *The Clock* is made of a twenty-four-hour montage of thousands of time-related scenes from movies, edited and shown in "real time." Each clip contains the time on a clock or watch or in a clip of dialogue when people refer to the time. There are shots of sundials from black-and-white movies; a clip from *Easy Rider* where Peter Fonda looks at his watch (showing 11:40 a.m.), then throws it away; and the "Alas poor Yorick" scene from Olivier's *Hamlet*, when a distant bell tolls the quarter hour. *The Clock* is synchronized so that whatever time is shown is the correct time in the "real world." The film is a gigantic and completely impractical clock. The viewer is encouraged to think about the nature of time in the cinema and in life. *The Clock* is a masterpiece that will run and run, without ever needing to be wound, because it's powered by a strong idea. Marclay has little technical skill to marvel at; it's his concepts that are hugely impressive. Our minds remember powerful ideas long after they have forgotten impressive skill.

Creative thinking is about vision, awareness and expression. Skill is useful, but not essential. It's important to avoid the trap of wanting to impress people with skill, and it's easy to confuse this with ability. Ability is about your innate sensibility and understanding. Skill is about training and repetition. Is the great opera singer who forces herself to practice for hours each day expressing a love of music, or merely exploiting a skill? Enjoying music for the sake of it is rewarding. The creative mind explores whatever it is fascinated by rather than build up an armory of skills.

Running a large and successful business requires a high level of skill to deal with balance sheets, business management, finance and accounting. Or does it? Sir Richard Branson, the founder of the multimillion-dollar Virgin Group, is a case in point. His poor math skills were once exposed in a board meeting when Virgin's director realized that Branson didn't understand the difference between net and gross profit. The director drew a sea, then fishes in a net (profit) and some fishes outside (turnover). Branson understood the math when it had been transformed into a visual image. He was surprised and disappointed—he'd thought it was the other way round—and realized Virgin wasn't making as much money as he'd thought. Knowing the difference between net and gross is an elementary business skill, yet without it he had created an empire with sixty thousand employees. Branson's lack of math skills was an advantage—because he didn't get caught up in financial details he could see the big picture. He had other people to do the math. Branson may have no business skill, but he does have an ability for business—a gut instinct for what the public wants and how to deliver it.

A lack of skill and expertise had prevented a student in one of my workshops from fulfilling his lifetime dream of opening a restaurant. We came up with the idea of a takeout restaurant— a restaurant without a kitchen, where customers could order from the menus of nearby takeout joints and have their food delivered to their table. My student had no restaurant experience or skills, but in this way he was able to open a restaurant. Eventually he and his colleagues had built up enough resources to hire a chef and kitchen equipment and slowly begin to serve their own recipes.

When someone emphasizes technique rather than the concept, it is proof that they have run out of ideas. The genuinely creative are not seeking to display skill but have a sincere interest in understanding and expressing ideas about their subject. Those with mechanical minds seek perfect technique by asking "How?" But those with curiosity seek understanding by asking "Why?"

SOMETIMES INCOMPETENCE IS USEFUL. IT HELPS
YOU KEEP AN OPEN MIND.

— Roberto Cavalli

More? Be a beginner forever on page 4.

maintain momentum

When F. Scott Fitzgerald had an idea for a story, he completely
devoted himself to developing it. Fitzgerald wrote and rewrote
his stories repeatedly. He lived and breathed the tale and
worked on the narrative every day without a break until it was
finished, relentlessly rereading and editing his work over and
over again, day after day. He explained this as stubbornness. As
a result, complex sentences gallop like wild horses in all directions in his work, but always with Fitzgerald's firm hand on the
reins. The reader senses that he writes when on fire, in the
zone. Writing and rewriting the stories intensified his unique
voice. He wrote in a way that was uniquely his own. He honed
each sentence to perfection.

A great idea is electrifying and exhilarating. It has energy.
But no matter how strong the idea, if you sit on it, it gets cold.

You must maintain the sense of excitement you had when first inspired. Whatever the project—building a house extension, renovating a boat or planning to open a store—it's important to ride the momentum. Work on an idea constantly until it's resolved. The minute we lose momentum, we lose the thread. Our inner critic awakens. We start doubting what we're doing and energy levels drop. When it comes to creative execution, the key is to get moving—and keep moving.

> FROM THE BEGINNING OF QUEEN THERE WAS
> SUCH MOMENTUM THAT I NEVER HAD ANY
> TIME TO DO ANYTHING ELSE. MY ENERGY WAS
> NINETY-FIVE PERCENT FOCUSED ON THE BAND.
>
> *—Brian May*

Meet one writer who wouldn't give up on page 39, and another who took it easy on page 124.

make the present a present

Our ability to immerse ourselves in the present, and to live in the moment, is one we must nurture. The composer Maurice

Ravel realized this during his extraordinary experiences in World War II. Deployed as a truck driver, Ravel was never safe from the relentless artillery shells, enemy snipers, poison gas and machine-gun fire as he zigzagged along cratered roads supplying the front lines. In winter, the ground froze hard. In spring, rain turned the battlefields to mud. Soldiers' feet swelled to three times their normal size in the water, which often turned them gangrenous and resulted in amputation. Rats grew to the size of dogs by feeding off the rotting corpses littering no-man's-land. The stench of open latrines and rotting bodies was inescapable. Ravel suffered exposure, frostbite and dysentery. The deafening noise made his ears ring even during the rare moments of silence.

Early one sunny morning, Ravel was driving down roads lined with dead, blasted trees, through bleak, bombed-out towns. The light was crisp and clear, and in the distance he saw a wrecked château. Inside he miraculously discovered an Erard piano in perfect condition. He sat and played some Chopin, and the surrounding horror melted away. He created an ecstatic, exhilarating moment for himself. He became fully involved in the music and immersed himself in the present, later describing it as one of the highlights of his life.

How was Ravel able to shut out the surrounding horror of war? Reading Ravel's letters and accounts by his friends reveals that he understood his thinking and moods. He controlled his own thoughts and feelings rather than letting them control him. Many people believe that their thoughts are something that happen to them, instead of something they are making happen. Ravel, though, understood the workings of his mind and the fact that he was manufacturing his own moods. He could create an emotional distance from his surroundings and focus on the here and now. He didn't allow past regrets and future concerns to ruin the present. Instead, he harnessed his art to transport him. It's a skill we can all learn, with practice.

Ravel wrote some of his most popular works, such as *Le Tombeau de Couperin*, in the midst of war. He turned his traumatic surroundings and experiences into something positive. Ravel believed that the purpose of life was to taste experiences, whether good or bad, and reach out for newer and richer ones. Pleasure is not over there but here. Not in the future, but now.

It's important to adore what you do, and become totally immersed in it. The psychologist Mihaly Csikszentmihalyi explains, "Flow is being completely involved in an activity for its own sake. The ego falls away. Time flies. Every action, movement, and thought follows inevitably from the previous one, like playing jazz."

Wherever you are and whatever you do, strive to become totally engrossed. When you are truly immersed in whatever you're experiencing, whether beautiful or ugly, good or bad, your present circumstances don't dictate your destination— they only determine your departure point.

Yes? Seize the moment and maintain momentum on page 68.
No? Take a year off to get back on track on page 81.

be mature enough to be childish

Steve Jobs was astonished. As CEO of Apple he'd given young start-up design group Hovey-Kelley their big break, a commission that could have established their reputation. Apple had set the standard for elegant design, yet the Hovey-Kelley people presented him with something that looked like a bunch of five-year-olds had produced it in playschool. Assorted scraps, a ball from a roll-on deodorant, a piece of a refrigerator, bits of a car gearshift and a dish from a supermarket, all held together with tape and rubber bands.

David Kelley and his colleagues were grown men with a business to run, and they'd spent days playing like children. They played around with scraps of objects and playschool materials. They'd had a lot of fun, but then they had to present the result to Jobs, with his notoriously high standards.

In the early 1980s, products were formally designed in detailed drawings and then fabricated to these specifications. It was a lengthy and sophisticated process. Very grown-up, very serious. Kelley didn't want to work that way. It was too slow and restrictive. He wanted to play around with whatever materials were on hand and make a prototype quickly.

It was a crude creation, but it visualized an idea quickly. Jobs instantly understood what this mishmash of bits and pieces meant. It was a revolutionary new computer mouse. It was one of the most sophisticated yet accessible pieces of technology ever made. Previous versions of the mouse could only be moved in a linear up, down and across motion, were full of fussy little parts and were very expensive to make. The basic principle in Kelley's prototype, pairing a freely rolling ball (the roll-on deodorant) with an optoelectronic system, would be used by generations of mice. Billions were made. Due to its success, Hovey-Kelley blossomed into IDEO, the renowned international design consultancy.

How do you get adults to take play seriously? When giving a lecture, I've often tried an experiment made famous by Bob McKim, an eminent researcher into creativity in the 1970s (he was a big influence on IDEO). I give everyone a pen and paper and ask them to draw the person next to them, then show each other their drawings. The reaction is always embarrassed laughter and repeated apologies.

McKim felt this proved how much we fear others' judgment. We're embarrassed about showing our ideas, and this apprehension makes us unadventurous. Contrast this with the reaction of children undertaking the same exercise. They demonstrate a complete lack of inhibition. They're confident to show their work to anyone. Studies show that when children are in a secure environment they feel most free to play. The same is true of adults.

My main role as a university instructor and as a creative consultant is to set up a situation where people feel confident enough to be playful. Being playful is what enables us to develop. When organizations tell me they aren't generating enough ideas and are falling behind their competitors, it's usually because their people are fearful and insecure. Scared of what their boss or colleagues will think; scared they'll get it "wrong."

Artists like Jean Dubuffet in the 1940s led the way in reappraising the value of play. He was fascinated by the sense of freedom expressed in children's art. It was generally dismissed as worthless and primitive, but Dubuffet saw it as fresh and unself-conscious. He didn't simply copy the style of children's art; he copied their raw, innocent approach. He realized that although there were many benefits to maturity, he had forgotten one essential ingredient of creativity: play.

Dubuffet resolved to return to the unfettered mindset of childhood when he was working. His paintings became full of the life, savage energy and inventiveness of the child. He worked with the unprejudiced joy of an infant trying out everything, fascinated by everything. Despite his work receiving the "a child of five could do that" jibes from critics, Dubuffet eventually gained an international reputation and a place in art history. The mindset of a child helped him to stay young, both emotionally and mentally, even into old age.

A firm plagued by executive burnout called me in to see if I could prevent their best managers from suffering mental exhaustion. Stress leave was costing the company millions in lost productivity. The executives told me that packed schedules, deadlines and responsibility meant the job was no fun anymore. I asked them to list fun activities, and then I asked them to list how long they took. The executives discovered that most of their enjoyable activities took a day or longer. They weren't having fun because they didn't have enough time to fit them in. We broke the activities down into short mini-breaks of half an hour or less. Suddenly there were outlets for fun at many points during the day. Stress levels plummeted, production soared, and more importantly, the executives felt more fulfilled in both their working and private lives.

The future belongs to those who can reconnect with play. It is the child in you that is creative, not the adult. The child is free and does not know what he or she can't or shouldn't do. The child hasn't found what works, whereas adults repeat whatever worked last time. Whatever you are doing, do it as if for the first time.

THERE ARE CHILDREN PLAYING IN THE STREETS
WHO COULD SOLVE SOME OF MY TOP PROBLEMS
IN PHYSICS, BECAUSE THEY HAVE MODES OF
SENSORY PERCEPTION THAT I LOST LONG AGO.

— *Robert Oppenheimer*

Still need cheering up? Stay playful on page 178.

aspire to have no goals

Cut up this page with a pair of scissors. Slice up some words and sentences. Shuffle them and then rearrange them in a way that completely changes the original meaning. You will find that extraordinary things happen; unpredictable and unusual phrases will fall into place. You are freed from the usual structures and purposes of writing and are led in all sorts of mind-expanding directions.

A goal defines the outcome. When you have a goal, the route to it becomes a chore. The imagination becomes closed to other possibilities. If the process is interesting, the result will be interesting. The creative explore in a truly open and experimental way; they don't start with a destination in mind, because a target would trap them on a predetermined path. The search for an objective becomes a barrier to real creativity and exploration. Go out looking for one thing, and that's all you'll ever find. A moth has a goal, the flame, but it is then consumed by it.

The writer who best exemplifies this is William Burroughs. He became one of the most influential authors of modern culture because he didn't set out with a clear goal in mind when starting a novel. He used a cut-up technique to create an alternative to traditional, linear narratives. When he started a novel, he had no idea what it would be about or who the characters would be. Sentences from a newspaper, book or other piece of writing were sliced up and then pasted back together, often at random. Burroughs's process constantly threw up unusual combinations and surprising phrases, which kept him excited and engaged in his writing. Unexpected pathways opened up to him. Burroughs freed himself from the conventions and representational straitjacket of the linear novel, and in doing so became a literary phenomenon.

If you don't know where you're going, the journey is more surprising and your work is more enriching. The highest purpose is to have no purpose at all. The drive toward achievements is important, but rather than identifying goals it is better to identify areas of focus. A goal is a result; an area of focus is a gateway. Don't plan how to work, just work.

YOU ARE LOST THE INSTANT YOU KNOW WHAT
THE RESULT WILL BE.

— *Cubist painter Juan Gris*

Find out more about how doing nothing can achieve great things on page 80.

Open your mind

Andy Warhol's open mind was reflected in the way his studio operated. The door was always open. Anyone could walk in off the street and talk to him, make suggestions or even help make the artworks. There was no privacy. There were no individual working areas. Everything was open for all to see.

A large group of creative individuals slowly formed in his studio, drawn by this attitude of openness. They helped with Warhol's work, suggesting ideas for paintings and even producing them. It was an exciting creative atmosphere where people felt free to contribute ideas, without judgment or hierarchy. Many felt for the first time in their lives the freedom to truly be themselves. The studio became a hub for all kinds of experimental art, including the rock band the Velvet Underground and Lou Reed.

The benefits of the way Warhol's studio operated were so clear that they have been copied extensively in the art world. Jeff Koons, Anselm Kiefer, Damien Hirst and others have all adopted his operating methods. And, while Warhol's studio may seem as if it was only possible in the art world, its influence has in fact permeated much deeper; his system also filtered through to design companies and to more traditional businesses.

Many of the companies that function most successfully have adopted a similar flat structure, allowing employees to own a piece of the company, making them genuinely committed to the cause. They have few or no levels of middle management between staff and executives. Workers are more productive when directly involved in decision-making, rather than being closely supervised by middle management. Creativity thrives in a workplace or studio that is open to possibilities and new ideas, no matter how crazy they might appear, where invention will not be laughed at but taken seriously. An open studio creates open minds. And to an open mind there are multiple solutions.

THE BARRIERS ARE NOT ERECTED WHICH CAN
SAY TO ASPIRING TALENTS AND INDUSTRY,
"THUS FAR AND NO FURTHER."

—Ludwig van Beethoven

More? Discover why janitors love working at Pixar on page 129, and why Bill Gates doesn't mind the right thing being in the wrong place on page 98.

Pause for thoughtlessness

There is an art to doing nothing, intensely. The geniuses of the twenty-first century will be those who can unplug from the unyielding flow of incoming communication: emails, texts, tweets, Facebook, phone calls, and on and on. There's no hiding place from screens; we work at them, they entertain us; there are screens by escalators, in schools and in our pockets to fill the gaps when we are not looking at stationary screens. Genius is so rare today because we are so distracted, updated and connected. Rather than steering life we're reacting to whatever pours in. To work intensively for long periods you need to switch off occasionally for short periods.

Degas, Monet and other Impressionist painters often

worked intensively with strong colors in strong sunlight from dawn to dusk. They developed a technique of taking a five-minute break by looking into "black mirrors" made from the stone obsidian. This soothed their eyes and gave their conscious minds a break. They found that although they were not consciously thinking about the work, the machinery of their minds continued whirring. They returned to work refreshed and energized. They discovered that their eyes saw more and their fingers felt more. Everything seemed richer. They were totally in the moment. No memories pulled them backward and no plans pulled them forward. The answers to the problems they had been struggling with would suddenly become clear.

Working 24/7 is the Western way; we're all ambitious and want to succeed. It feels wrong to stop, even for a moment. It's counterintuitive, but shutting a business down for a year may be the best way to grow it. Every seven years designer Stefan Sagmeister shuts down his studio for twelve months. "Everything that we designed in the seven years following the first sabbatical had its roots in thinking done during that sabbatical," he has said. Simon Cohen, the founder of Global Tolerance, also made the counterintuitive choice to place his entire communications agency on a one-year sabbatical. Global Tolerance had grown rapidly, gained high-profile clients and was highly successful. Cohen decided the company needed a rest and time to reflect, which was only going to be possible by taking a year out. Logistically, it wasn't easy. "Our HR people said there was no such thing as a company sabbatical. It had never been done before," he said. They made arrangements to prevent their clients from being stolen by competitors, and after a year they came back stronger and better.

If you're a manager, allow employees to take a day or a week off. If you're a corporate leader, use a sabbatical system to refresh your team. If you're self-employed, force yourself to do nothing from time to time. We tend not to value shutting down, but it's more than just an absence of work; it's a tool for recovery. It's important to completely clear your mind. Only when you achieve this can you begin again, refreshed. To think deeply, sometimes you first have to empty your mind.

NOW AND THEN IT'S GOOD TO PAUSE IN OUR
PURSUIT OF HAPPINESS AND JUST BE HAPPY.

—Guillaume Apollinaire

Still not convinced? Mine your mind for your breakthrough idea on page 131.

Plan to have more accidents

You spill a cup of coffee over your work; your pen leaks, or the printer goes crazy. It happens to everyone. Don't automatically discard accidents, but instead work with them. Go along with them and see where they lead. Use them to propel yourself forward in unexpected directions.

The problem is not the accident; the problem is you. Override your preprogrammed and preconceived ideas that accidents are something going wrong. Be more receptive to the unexpected. The painter Francis Bacon summed up the creative person's attitude to chance: "All painting is an accident. But it's also not an accident, because one must select what part of the accident one chooses to preserve."

In everyday life we all try to avoid accidents in our work. Far from being annoyed by accidents, however, creative people are intrigued by them. The most successful scientists have not thought like scientists—in a logical, linear way—but more like artists. If something goes "wrong," they look for the "right" in it.

Édouard Bénédictus accidentally knocked a glass beaker from a shelf. The beaker broke. Surprisingly, it didn't shatter into small shards but broke into just a few large pieces. As well as being a composer, writer and painter, Bénédictus was widely curious, so he investigated. He discovered that the beaker had contained cellulose nitrate, which had held the shards of glass together. He quickly spotted the potential of glass that broke but didn't shatter; his safety glass first appeared in World War I gas masks, then in windshields, and soon became ubiquitous.

Vulcanized rubber was discovered by accident by Charles Goodyear. Rubber was too soft when hot and too brittle when cold. Goodyear accidentally spilled some rubber on his stove. It baked into a hard, dark substance, strong and pliable at any temperature. He had discovered the process of vulcanization by accident, but he used the accident to his advantage. He is considered to be the patron saint of inventors because these days rubber is present in almost every mechanical object.

The electric current was discovered by accident by Galvani, as was immunology by Pasteur, X-rays by Röntgen, photography by Daguerre, radioactivity by Becquerel and penicillin by Fleming.

Become a student of the University of Accidents. When they invented the computer, they also invented the computer crash. The printer, the blotchy print. Every technology carries with it the potential for accidents. Work with them and explore them. Accidents generate new perspectives. They appeal to the creative mind because we live in an imperfect world—we are imperfect and our work is imperfect.

Accidents reflect reality more accurately than does perfection. Perfection is the aberration. Think of an accident as an answer in search of a different question. Work out what that question is. It is probably more interesting than the one you were asking.

THERE IS NO SUCH THING AS ACCIDENT; IT IS
FATE MISNAMED.

—*Napoléon Bonaparte*

Inspired? Embrace the art of imperfection on page 50, or read on to meet the world's most successful failure.

If you can't be really good, be really bad

I've watched the films of Ed Wood over and over again. *Bride of the Monster, Plan 9 from Outer Space* and *Night of the Ghouls* are unbelievable. Unbelievably bad. They were some of the poorest-quality and also some of the strangest films ever made. The critics lashed every film Wood released, and they were all box-office failures, but his zeal for making movies remained undimmed. Wood created a remarkable number of films. He raised the capital, produced, wrote, directed and acted in them, often simultaneously. On film after film he worked with the reckless enthusiasm of a child, with nothing dampening his spirit. You forgive even his worst films because he still manages to convey his love for the trashy characters, plots and sets.

Lesser men, if forced to make movies under the conditions Wood faced, would have given up.

Wood's posthumous fame began when he was awarded the accolade of "Worst Director of All Time" in 1980, just two years after his death. Today, his films are celebrated for their technical mistakes, wobbly sets, unsophisticated special effects, eccentric dialogue, peculiar casts and bizarre plots. These features add charm, character and a zany spirit that are more lasting and enduring than the blockbusters churned out by Hollywood. Wood's beguiling films have the rare attributes of sincerity and humanity that most high-tech, high-budget sci-fi films lack. They were produced for a pittance with untrained actors, and you sense that everyone involved was driven by commitment, not money.

Something badly done can be refreshing. Being uncool or nerdy can be charming. It's a way of showing that you don't care what anyone else thinks. The world is full of people who dedicate their lives to seeking approval. They chase after vindication from others and lose themselves in the process. Aiming for critical credibility or commercial success can be vastly more limiting than relying on passion and enthusiasm, the engines that power creativity.

AuctionWeb was a bad website. People posted badly lit, unfocused photos of junk they wanted to sell. A 24/7 worldwide garage sale. It was horrible to scroll through the visually appalling photos. One of the first items sold was a broken laser pointer for $14.83. Astonished, the founder of the site, Pierre Omidyar, emailed the winning bidder to ask if he understood that the laser pointer was broken. The buyer explained in his reply, "I'm a collector of broken laser pointers." That's when Omidyar realized he was on to something.

He had founded AuctionWeb in California in 1995. It soon changed its name to eBay. eBay became one of the great new technology companies of the last twenty-five years *because* it was bad and unashamedly uncool. Omidyar poured his enthusiasm into it and made it work well, but he didn't try to make it chic or sophisticated.

Too much self-criticism can paralyze you and stop you from moving forward. People with mediocre ideas and poor taste often achieve exceptional success because they don't know when to stop. Better the errors of enthusiasm than the slick competence of the cool.

SUCCESS IS THE ABILITY TO GO FROM FAILURE
TO FAILURE WITHOUT LOSING YOUR
ENTHUSIASM.

— *Winston Churchill*

Disagree? Discover the merits of feeling inadequate on page 27.

raise the dead

Can you guess which film is described below?

An orphaned boy, our hero, lives with his aunt and uncle in the middle of nowhere. Their life is unexciting and he longs for something more.

Our hero's life is turned upside down one day when a strange character arrives to tell him the truth about his background, parents and true potential. He discovers that his parents were special and that he too can learn special powers.

A bearded, elderly guardian, who knows his full history but is not prepared to reveal everything, mentors our hero. The guardian rescued him as a baby and delivered him to his aunt and uncle to hide the child from evil forces.

The boy is taught to use his extraordinary powers; he manifests them through a special stick. Only select people have these powers, which enable them to do extraordinary things.

Our hero learns that there exists an embodiment of evil, who murdered his parents. He is the master of dark powers; he intends to rule the world and will do anything to make that happen. His minions work hard to spread his evil.

Our hero declares that he will never be tempted by the power of evil and sets out on a quest to destroy it. Along the way he befriends two loyal, trusted sidekicks, one male—emotional and headstrong—and the other female—smart and astute. Later they fall in love with each other. Our hero overcomes immense dangers to save his friends, and we begin to realize the great future ahead of him.

In the end, the embodiment of evil is defeated by a greater power—love.

It could be *Star Wars* or Harry Potter. With a bit of tweaking it could be a lot of other films too. The similarity doesn't diminish their power or, strangely, their originality. I'm a huge fan of *Star Wars* and have watched it tens of times. My loft is full of the original toys. I am a big fan of Harry Potter and have watched the films tens of times. My loft is full of the original toys. I waited in line with my children late at night to get the books on first release, have read them several times and have spent many hours listening to the audiotapes read by Stephen Fry. I never tired of the storyline, even though I already knew it from *Star Wars*.

All creative work builds on what has gone before. When someone declares that something is original, it's because they are unaware of the influences. The creative make the most of things they admire and aren't ashamed to be inspired by something they respect. The bad news: everything has already been done. The good news: it can be done again.

The plot of Stephenie Meyer's *Twilight* was inspired by *Wuthering Heights*, but quickly deviates from Emily Brontë's classic. *Wide Sargasso Sea* by Jean Rhys was a creative response to Charlotte Brontë's *Jane Eyre*. Rhys was so entranced by the book that she created a prequel that fills in the characters' backstories and gives the character Bertha a voice that she lacked in the original. Stravinsky cut up the music of Pergolesi and Tchaikovsky, and the folk music that he loved, and collaged them into new work.

If the action of *Moby-Dick* by Herman Melville was set today, what would it be like? Swap the white whale for a white shark and you can see where the inspiration for Peter Benchley's novel and Steven Spielberg's film *Jaws* originated. They took a classic and pushed it further.

"*Jaws* on a spaceship." That was all Ridley Scott said when he pitched the film *Alien* to producers at 20th Century Fox. That was all he needed to say. There are numerous similarities, but Ridley Scott and his team transformed the core idea of *Jaws* into something unique and original as they added their own concepts. *Jaws* was the scaffolding Scott used to build his own house. *Alien* has spawned a hundred copies, and so it goes on.

If work by someone else really gets into your head, sometimes you have to reinvent it yourself, simply to get it back out of your head.

THERE IS NO HARM IN REPEATING A GOOD THING.

—*Plato*

Not interested in reworking your own ideas? Rework your idols' on page 138.

be a conservative revolutionary

An elegant model strutted down the catwalk in high heels. She wore a gracefully tailored white dress puffed out by a cotton tulle underdress. The audience contained the fashion world's most elite representatives. They were stunned when, halfway down the catwalk, the model was attacked from both sides. Colored paint was sprayed across her dress in overlapping streaks. The model's face was spattered and paint dribbled down her dress onto the floor. Why?

It was all staged by the enfant terrible of fashion design, Alexander McQueen, for his spring/summer collection. The audience literally screamed their ovation, and dress no. 13, spring/summer 1999, is now a fashion icon.

It's important not to do the same old things in the same old way, but to push them to the limit and see what happens.

McQueen was the most iconic and celebrated fashion designer of the 1990s. His mesmerizing outfits and otherworldly designs became instant classics—but McQueen amplified his impact by transforming fashion shows into performance art. Instead of simply marching models up and down a catwalk, McQueen's shows were sensational events, with rain pouring onto the catwalk, wolves terrorizing the audience, fire leaping from the floor, models ice-skating, models as ethereal holograms in glass pyramids, re-creations of shipwrecks and mental asylums. He turned fashion shows into unmissable events.

The American painter Mark Rothko was similarly excessive. His first one-man exhibition in New York featured portraits of his friends. They were ordinary. So he began to push painting to the limit. He put all his efforts into what he was good at—shape, color and composition. His paintings became more and more abstract. Eventually he and the other Abstract Expressionists started producing paintings that were *entirely* abstract, an expression of pure feeling and nothing more. Until then, paintings had always been based on something in the real world.

Rothko developed paintings based on rectangular blocks of two to three complementary colors. The blocks vibrate and resonate against the surrounding area. The monumental canvases overwhelm and completely envelop the viewer. His paintings express basic human emotions—tragedy, ecstasy and doom. Viewers often describe feeling something close to the deep spiritual experience Rothko claimed to have had while painting them.

Many people never connect with their real talents and fail to attain their potential because they don't push what they do to excess. Creativity is like mining; we need to dig deep to discover and uncover ourselves.

Whatever your field, push your work to the limit. One person who is willing to be excessive can achieve more in an hour than fifty reasonable people can achieve in a year.

IF YOU AREN'T IN OVER YOUR HEAD, HOW DO
YOU KNOW HOW TALL YOU ARE?

—*T. S. Eliot*

Meet another conservative revolutionary who was full of contradictions on page 91.

Work the hours that work for you

Scientists in the Theoretical Division of the Los Alamos National Laboratory were troubled when their brilliant colleague Mitchell Feigenbaum began living by a twenty-six-hour clock instead of the traditional twenty-four-hour one. His days went in and out of phase with theirs—he periodically woke up to a setting sun, or had breakfast when they were having supper.

Feigenbaum was studying chaos and wanted randomness in everyday life. During his twenty-six-hour day he didn't think about traditional scientific problems; he thought about clouds, and the smoke swirls from cigarettes and whirlpools, which were structured yet unpredictable. His colleagues thought he was wasting his gifts, but he became the man most responsible for chaos theory, the study of randomness in a system that also obeys laws. No other recent theoretical science has had such a phenomenal impact on our culture.

Chaos posed problems that flouted established scientific methods. Only someone like Feigenbaum, who thought and lived differently, could have cracked its code.

The writer Craig Clevenger seals himself in his house for days when starting a new novel. He covers the clocks and windows in order to lose all sense of the passage of time. Nobel Prize–winning writer Toni Morrison starts writing before dawn. Charles Dickens walked the streets of London at night and met strange characters who resurfaced in his novels.

Routine behavior leads to routine thinking. If you're engrossed in your work, you become lost in the moment and perform at your peak. Work the hours that work for you.

IF YOU WANT TO CHANGE YOUR ART, CHANGE YOUR HABITS.

— Clement Greenberg

Not quite convinced? Become immersed in the moment on page 69.

Search without finding

I watched the most mysterious and enigmatic man I've ever seen stride across the room. He emerged from nowhere and was going nowhere. His thin limbs seemed to stretch out endlessly and gave him a fragile appearance, yet he exuded inner strength. Six feet tall, he leaned forward with determination and seemed knowing, yet tentative and questioning. A universal man encapsulating our times.

Walking Man 1 was a 1960 bronze sculpture by Alberto Giacometti that strode into the record books in 2010 when it sold for $104.3 million. Giacometti was an artist who felt he could never capture another person in paint or plaster because people were too unfathomable and complex. When painting or sculpting, Giacometti searched but never found. More importantly, he enjoyed that state of ignorance. There was more freedom in it than knowing, than being certain. He worked from real life, yet he was wise enough to understand that he could only ever try to, but never truly, capture reality.

Don't be ashamed of being ignorant. Ignorance is natural. Creativity exists in not knowing. You have to be happy to admit that you are ignorant and may never find a solution. Be willing to look stupid, to risk the emotional pain of getting it wrong.

When the Delphic oracle declared the philosopher Socrates the wisest person in Greece, he suggested that it was because he realized how little he knew. He also realized how little every-one else knew! Socrates didn't have a philosophy and didn't write anything down; he simply asked his followers questions. He considered it a success if, at the end of a session with him, his followers knew less than at the beginning.

If you don't know what you're doing, you don't know what you can't do. Use what you've learned to create a higher-quality ignorance. Embrace your not-knowing and stride forward with determination and uncertainty.

PAINTING TO ME IS CONSTANT SEARCHING. I
CAN SEE WHAT I WANT, BUT I CAN'T GET THERE,
AND YET YOU HAVE TO BE OPEN ENOUGH THAT
IF IT GOES ANOTHER WAY, THEN LET IT GO
THAT WAY.

—*Jamie Wyeth*

More? Embrace the certainty of doubt on page 25.

don't overlook the overlooked

After reading a newspaper account of the murder of farmer Herbert Clutter, his wife and children in 1959, writer Truman

Capote decided to investigate. He made the thousand-mile journey to the crime scene, a picturesque and tranquil farmhouse outside a small town in Kansas. The Clutters were decent, hardworking and gentle. The killers were the dark side of America: rootless, impetuous and irreverent. This contrast fascinated Capote. He wanted to understand as deeply as possible the motives and characters of everyone involved. He saturated himself in the incident, interviewing local residents, police appointed to the case and the killers before their executions. After six years he had compiled eight thousand pages of notes, which became the basis for his award-winning nonfiction classic *In Cold Blood*.

The book was an instant sensation and is now considered a masterpiece of American reportage. Indeed, Capote created a new genre, an original form: the "nonfiction novel." It was neither a whodunnit nor a will-they-be-caught because those questions were answered at the beginning. Instead, its fascination lay in other things: getting into the minds of those involved and discovering what made them tick; exploring the dynamics between the murderers and their victims; and the suspense of reading to the end to find out the gory details.

The intriguing and compelling surround us, but we often don't notice them. There are reports of murders in most newspapers, most days. We flick through them and they barely register. Creativity can be as simple as seizing on something that has been overlooked by the world and forcing the world to take notice.

If your mind is alert to your surroundings and the

strangeness in the commonplace, you can make the most of whatever is already out there. Use anything interesting that you find.

Find natural inspiration in the everyday on page 34.

Put the right thing in the wrong place

How can you refresh your perspective and see things in a new light? Put something or someone in an unusual place. Looking at your subject in an unexpected location throws off the preconceptions and stereotypes you have of that subject, revealing its extraordinary potential.

Surrealist artists invented the simple technique of putting two different objects together to create unusual juxtapositions. During the 1930s, Salvador Dalí created a number of surreal objects that would change the nature of product design. The most famous of these is the lobster telephone, in which a replica lobster replaced the receiver. It was fully functioning. Dalí understood that everyday things had a meaning beyond their practical function. We are surrounded by objects that are the legacy of his vision of combining unusual objects, from phones shaped like burgers or bananas, to baby strollers—the latter another reminder that putting two unusual objects together can unleash huge potential.

Owen Maclaren designed the undercarriage of the Spitfire, the British fighter plane that dominated the skies during the Battle of Britain. Its undercarriage folded up in a neat but complex way. In 1965 Maclaren invented a collapsible stroller inspired by this folding mechanism, and it revolutionized the transportation of babies and small children; previously, carriages and strollers had been heavy, rigid and impractical. Owen went into production with the new lightweight aluminum Maclaren Baby Buggy in 1967. It sold millions in dozens of countries. Maclaren also inspired other collapsible objects, such as the Strida bicycle.

At Microsoft, Bill Gates liked to transfer employees to completely different departments for a while, to see what new ideas might result. Sometimes it produced nothing, but occasionally it produced amazing results.

Put disparate people and things together, and see what happens.

THE MAN WHO CANNOT VISUALISE A HORSE
GALLOPING ON A TOMATO IS AN IDIOT.

—*André Breton*

Inspired? Try going from A to B via Z on page 168.

Stay hungry

We crave luxury, but it's a motivational sedative. It's a hindrance. It saps us of incentive. It whispers to our unconscious mind to relax, to take it easy. Neutral, simple, humble spaces are what help us to focus. Luxury is not for the creative; it's for poodles.

The most uncompromising portrait painter of his era, Lucian Freud, kept his studio bare, empty and free of distractions. Freud forged his closest bonds in his studio. His sitters—duchesses, drag queens, queens, his partners and children—never forgot the intense experience. There was nothing else to concentrate on other than the experience of painting and being painted.

To get to the truth, Freud needed a pared-down environment. In his studio all his models, however beautiful or grotesque, were subjected to the same austere interrogation. He painted them as he saw them, describing blemishes and flaws with none of the customary flattery of portrait painters. He invested everything in the painting, without relying on creature comforts of any kind.

Freud worked long hours, seven days a week, all year round. He cut himself off from the clamor of the city. He stayed alert and fresh because he was isolated from the distractions of everyday life.

Freud did not lead a monastic life. At a drinking club called the Colony Room, for every sip I took of my drink, he'd down a glass. He frequently got into fights. He had a lot of children with many different partners. He lived life to the fullest. It was different in his studio, though; there he needed a clear mental space.

Ralph Waldo Emerson, Emily Dickinson, Henry David Thoreau and others too numerous to mention have all sought solitude to find a rich vein of inspiration. A sparse office or studio keeps the brain sharp. The mind wants to wander. Keep it on track by eliminating sidetracks.

THE SADDEST THING I CAN IMAGINE IS TO GET USED TO LUXURY.

— *Charlie Chaplin*

See why Einstein favored a messy workspace on page 138.

Surprise yourself

You may not realize it, but you have an interesting story to tell. A must-hear tale. We all do. A struggle against illness, family hardship, poverty or a sudden breakthrough moment. Whether we are aware of it or not, our life is our subject matter, and freeing up our memories allows us to surprise ourselves and learn about our personalities and what makes us unique. Everything is self-expression; we create our biographies in everything we do.

Artist Frida Kahlo made the most of the events of her life. Her iconic, autobiographical paintings are technically crude, but they are fascinating because they tell her enthralling story. Her optimism and boundless enthusiasm were not affected by the tragic events of her life. At the age of six she was stricken with polio, which left her with a deformed foot and a limp. Later in life she suffered serious injuries to her right leg and pelvis in a traffic accident and faced a lifelong battle against pain. During her convalescence she painted her first self-portrait, the beginning of a lengthy series that mapped her emotional reactions to events in her life. Kahlo's injuries meant she could not have children, and she documented her miscarriages in paintings. She met the artist Diego Rivera and they embarked on a turbulent marriage. Kahlo underwent many operations on her spine and her crippled foot; at one point, threatened by gangrene, her right leg was amputated below the knee: a huge blow to someone so preoccupied with self-image. She learned to walk again with an artificial limb. All these events are chronicled in her paintings. She is her own subject matter.

Although Kahlo's later paintings became clumsy and chaotic due to the effects of pain, drugs and drink, they were her finest work, and her artistic reputation grew. The paintings show that she had decided not to be a victim. All the pain she suffered did not prevent her from having a love affair with life.

Howard Schultz is best known as the CEO of Starbucks. His father struggled with a series of blue-collar jobs, never able to find meaning or satisfaction in his work. Then he was injured at work and had no health insurance or worker's compensation. It left a lasting impression on Schultz. "It was not the calling of coffee, but the calling to try to build a company that my father never got a chance to work for," he has said. He believed Starbucks was the first company in America to offer comprehensive health insurance and ownership in the form of stock options to all of its employees. His negative experience proved to be positive for his company.

What makes you tick creatively? Like taking a clock apart to discover how it works, ask yourself, "What is the best idea I've ever had? What was my worst idea? What is my creative ambition?" Self-knowledge will help you to understand why you do things the way you do, what winds you up, what sets off your alarm bell. You'll start to understand the story you are trying to tell.

ALL ART IS AUTOBIOGRAPHICAL. THE PEARL IS
THE OYSTER'S AUTOBIOGRAPHY.

—Federico Fellini

Meet another artist who used her own experience to make an impression on page 17.

Suspend judgment

I sat in the Royal Albert Hall, along with a few thousand other music fans, completely riveted. Some had traveled hundreds of miles to be there. The historical setting contributed to the compelling atmosphere. The virtuoso pianist walked on stage, lifted the lid of his piano and sat there in silence for four minutes and thirty-three seconds with a seriousness of purpose that was palpable to us all. Then he closed the lid of the piano and walked off stage. We had listened excitedly to nothing. The audience and orchestra behind the pianist sat still; a violinist dropped his bow, an oboist rustled as he stretched his leg, and there was an unintentional wind solo from the stomach of a woman sitting two rows in front of me, but that was all. When the piece came to an end, the conductor said, "And now for some real music," and proceeded with the program of Brahms and Beethoven. What a philistine.

We had listened to John Cage's *4'33"*, a work that celebrates listening itself. Cage tried to eliminate judgment from music because he believed that everything was music, and that the sound of traffic was as beautiful as a Mozart concerto. Music didn't just exist in concert halls but was all around us, all the time.

To get the most out of any situation it is important to suspend judgment. We tend to judge everything—people, prices, products, behavior—and automatically categorize things as "good" or "bad." Once you have pigeonholed something, it is locked down. Deferring judgment keeps all possibilities open.

Try to abandon conventional criteria like the one that holds that traditional forms of art are more beautiful than anything else. Throw away hierarchies and accept that everything has qualities of some kind. Open yourself up to the beauty of all things.

Judgment and creativity are two different processes. It is important to create freely, and it is not possible to do that and judge at the same time. Defer forming opinions or jumping to conclusions until the end of the process.

LOOK. ART KNOWS NO PREJUDICE, ART KNOWS NO BOUNDARIES, AND ART DOESN'T REALLY HAVE JUDGMENT IN ITS PUREST FORM. SO JUST GO. JUST GO.

—*k.d. lang*

Convinced? Open your mind with Andy Warhol on page 78. Not convinced? Try searching high and low on page 128.

take advantage of a disadvantage

The extraordinary achievements of Chuck Close, the great photorealist artist, are a fascinating example of turning a disadvantage into an advantage. His huge, painstakingly accurate portrait paintings hang in every major museum in the world. The monumental scale is breathtaking. Standing before them is like standing in front of a mountain. The minute details astound and amaze, yet they pull together to make a towering portrait.

Catastrophe struck Close at the height of his fame. A blood clot in the spine left him paralyzed from the neck down. Close had been known for detailed brushwork, but suddenly he couldn't even hold a brush. As Jackson Pollock said, "Painting is no problem. The problem is what to do when you're not painting."

After intensive rehabilitation, Close regained slight movement in his arm. He learned to paint again with a paintbrush strapped to his wrist with tape. Eventually he could manipulate a brush well enough to create tiny abstract shapes. He went on to create an entirely new kind of portrait: small abstract squares that, viewed close up, are separate, swirling marks, but which seen from a distance coalesce like pixels into a single, mosaic-like, unified image. The colors were stronger and brighter. These paintings were even more popular than his earlier work and cemented Close's place in art history.

In 1980, the great jazz guitarist Pat Martino suffered a severe brain aneurysm and underwent an operation. The surgery led to complete amnesia; Martino couldn't remember his family and friends, how to play the guitar, his career, or even who he was. He felt he'd been "dropped cold, empty, neutral, cleansed . . . naked." For months he exhaustively studied his old recordings, and in time managed to reverse his memory loss and return to form on the guitar. His past recordings were "an old friend, a spiritual experience which remained beautiful and honest." In the early 1990s, he resumed performing, with a new dimension to his work.

Many regard Django Reinhardt as one of the greatest guitar players of all time because he invented an entirely new style of jazz called "hot" jazz guitar. He had to: three fingers on his left hand were burned and paralyzed in a fire. In overcoming this problem he created a musical tradition, and his most popular compositions have become jazz standards.

These creative thinkers not only overcame their disadvantages but actively used them to add a new depth to their work. Any setback can be an opportunity to begin again with more wisdom. "I must do something" always resolves more problems than "Something must be done."

ADVERSITY HAS THE EFFECT OF ELICITING

TALENTS, WHICH IN PROSPEROUS

CIRCUMSTANCES WOULD HAVE LAIN DORMANT.

—Horace

Prefer classical to jazz? Meet another musician who turned adversity to his advantage on page 133.

throw truth bombs

The truth has power, and therefore gives your work strength. It is often unpalatable—possibly even offensive. But revealing something that's hidden to most is the gift of true art.

The Impressionists revealed the truth about the optics of the eye and the perception of space. The futurists revealed the truth about how the modern world was all about speed, traveling quickly and information flowing swiftly. The surrealists revealed the truth about the importance of the subconscious and how our true desires were hidden from view. Pop Artists revealed the truth about the effects of consumer society and capitalism on our values. Conceptual artists revealed the truth about the dominance of ideas in our perception of the world. Galileo spent the latter years of his life under house arrest for revealing that the Earth was not the center of the universe but revolved round the sun. Darwin revealed that organisms evolve through natural selection. They were all searching for the real meaning of the world around them.

We live in a world of PR, image-makers, shifting identities and media consultants. Most people are trying to hide the truth, to cover things up and project a false image. The truly creative person seeks to reveal and not to conceal—to tell the truth about the truth. What is the real, below-the-surface reason you are interested in your subject?

ALL TRUTHS ARE EASY TO UNDERSTAND ONCE
THEY ARE DISCOVERED; THE POINT IS TO
DISCOVER THEM.

— *Galileo*

Inspired? Try shock and awe, page 111. Uninspired? Find out why the truth isn't always sufficient on page 185.

throw yourself into yourself

If you're not doing what you want, what are you doing?

The novelist James Joyce did not compromise—he wrote

in whatever way he wanted. He did not take into account the reader or the market potential of his writing. He made no concessions, staying true to his own unique style. The result was *Ulysses*, a turning point in modern literature. It presents the unedited, uncensored stream-of-consciousness thoughts of a fictitious character. There are long chaotic passages, strange words and obscure allusions. Many consider it the greatest book ever written. Others consider it the worst; it was even banned for many years. Whatever: the novel is exactly what Joyce wanted. He indulged himself and completely disregarded the readers and critics. He was not striving for something outside himself, such as critical acclaim or massive sales. He was not concerned with worldly ambitions, and this is why, paradoxically, *Ulysses* became an enduring classic.

Our society believes that work must be hard and unfulfilling. The things many of us really want to do—dance, act, paint, write—must be frivolous because they are enjoyable.

A student in one of my workshops was not doing what she wanted to do. She worked in the admin department of her company but wanted to work in the marketing department, producing ad campaigns. She had applied to transfer but had been frequently rebuffed. I explained that she needed to *show* them her potential. She created an entire campaign—came up with the concept, wrote the tagline, took the photos, designed the layouts, the whole shebang. She was transferred immediately.

We do our best work when we're having fun. Allow yourself to do what truly brings you joy. It's better for you. It's better for everyone. When you are satisfied, your satisfaction spreads to others.

> A MAN IS A SUCCESS IF HE GETS UP IN THE
> MORNING AND GOES TO BED AT NIGHT AND IN
> BETWEEN DOES WHAT HE WANTS TO DO.
>
> —*Bob Dylan*

More? Follow Robert De Niro and create your own opportunities on page 19.

Use shock and awe

The haphazard rows of razor-sharp teeth loomed out at me through the murky green liquid. I could see past them into the large black hole of its monstrous gullet. Its cold, black eyes stared at me and I stared back into the face of death.

I first saw *The Physical Impossibility of Death in the Mind of Someone Living* by Damien Hirst at the Saatchi Gallery in London in 1992. It was an artwork that dominated the era, a fourteen-foot real shark preserved in a huge glass tank filled with formaldehyde. The viewer stood a few inches away from its gaping jaws—a disturbingly immediate and visceral experience that brought you face-to-face with life and death. Hirst didn't want a painting of a shark. He wanted a real shark, real enough to frighten, to force the viewer out of his or her comfort zone. The work doesn't give you any choice; you are forced to confront your deepest fears.

In the creative world, stirring others out of their complacency can be good for everyone. The role of the scientist is generally to reassure, to establish certainty, to correct error. The role of the creative is to disturb, question and unsettle. The creative mind reveals deep, fundamental truths rather than mere facts.

When *Jaws* previewed in 1975, Steven Spielberg took a dose of Valium and stood anxiously at the back of a screening in Dallas. He flicked his gaze between the audience and the screen. After the scene where a boy on a raft is killed, a man in the front row stood up, ran out past Spielberg, threw up all over the carpet in the lobby, went to the bathroom to clean up and then returned to his seat. "That's when I knew I had a hit," said Spielberg.

If you don't have the attention of your audience, you're talking to yourself.

A vending machine in a shopping mall drew a great deal of attention; it displayed rows of shiny new pistols instead of chocolate bars or cans of soda. On close inspection, they turned out to be real. It was as easy to buy guns as snack food. The campaign, created by the Gun Control Alliance, a gun-free advocacy organization in South Africa, broke through the static to make its point. Of course you couldn't get a gun from the machine, but it made a real impact.

The real currency of our time isn't money—it's attention. You need people's attention in order to deliver a message of substance. New ideas will always shock. Don't let the reaction of others unnerve you.

THE SHOCK, EVEN DISGUST, PROVOKED BY THE
WORK IS PART OF ITS APPEAL.

—*Nicholas Serota*

More? Stand erect and make what you say unforgettable on page 148. Less? Let poor Rachmaninoff remind you that sometimes it takes longer than we'd like to be appreciated on page 116.

Value obscurity

If you feel overlooked, that no one is interested in what you're doing, enjoy the moment. Obscurity is a creative place: you are free to experiment and fail. No one is watching. No one has any expectations. Entrepreneurs, designers, writers and artists often make the most of the freedom obscurity offers.

Kurt Cobain and his band Nirvana recorded the multimillion-selling album *Nevermind*, one of the most influential records of all time, when they were virtually unknown. In obscurity, Cobain revelled in the thrill of finding his own voice, of creating a new language to speak to the world with. He experimented with guitar and vocal techniques just for the hell of it. Often homeless, he claimed he sometimes resorted to living under a bridge. It was a fraught but exciting time. He had all the time he needed to experiment and discover who he was and what he wanted to express.

After fame came his way, an army of people suddenly relied on Cobain: the other band members, the record company, managers, roadies, retailers, accountants, journalists, PAs and fans. Hundreds of magazines and TV stations clamored for interviews. They all wanted a stake in him. He quickly began to miss obscurity. Before the straitjacket of fame there was just Kurt, only one person to worry about. Now he bought an expensive mansion, but slept in a cheap motel nearby. He was trying to recapture the early sense of freedom. He wanted to develop, to experiment and try new ideas, but no one else wanted that. They wanted another *Nevermind*, and another, and another. Cobain came to realize that his anonymity had been precious.

If you're lucky enough to be in obscurity, make the most of it. Use your freedom to experiment, play, and stretch yourself.

Success brings the weight of expectations, and pressure that can do far more harm than good.

I'M AFRAID OF LOSING MY OBSCURITY.

GENUINENESS ONLY THRIVES IN THE DARK.

LIKE CELERY.

—*Aldous Huxley*

If you liked obscurity, you'll love anonymity on page 145. Alternatively, consider making yourself the story on page 32.

Value shared values

Robert Zimmerman felt cut off from the world. He grew up in the small town of Hibbing, Minnesota. No one there shared Zimmerman's interest in music, literature and art. No one really understood him. He knew he had to get out and find other creative people, so he moved to New York City, which was brimming with artists, writers, musicians and entrepreneurs. It was culture central, a focal point for new and exciting ideas. In New York his contemporaries fed him influences, shared discoveries and opened up the world to him—not just in music but in art and poetry. They shared new guitar chords and introduced him to the work of avant-garde poets, which influenced his lyrics. He changed his name to Bob Dylan, which symbolized his rebirth. The atmosphere drove Dylan to explore the boundaries of his talents. He felt more like himself than he ever had before.

A new friend introduced Dylan to the music of Woody Guthrie. The encounter was a revelation, making him realize that folk music could be a vehicle to communicate the thoughts and ideas that mattered most to him. He single-handedly ushered in the singer-songwriter era. Suddenly, what you sang about mattered more than how you sang it.

If it hadn't been for Sergey Rachmaninoff's friends, he would have given up early in his career. His powerful Symphony No. 1 was hated by both critics and the public when it was first performed, and was immediately deemed a failure. The experience had a terrible effect on the young composer, utterly destroying his confidence. Rachmaninoff lost the urge to compose and wrote nothing for the next three years. His friends set about nursing his fragile confidence back to full fitness; they loved his work and wanted to hear more. His desire to compose slowly returned, and he started work on his Piano Concerto No. 2. It was a success and restored the composer's confidence. But in all the years that followed he never attempted to have his first symphony published or performed again. It was a disaster that haunted him until his death.

During World War II the original score for Symphony No.

1 was discovered by accident and performed again. This time it was an extraordinary success and became one of the most respected of the twentieth century. Rachmaninoff, though, did not live to see its belated glory.

Find others who are on your wavelength and share your work. If you're a creative thinker, the chances are that you're challenging the accepted values and practices of the world around you. Gather a tribe of like-minded individuals to compare notes with and support one another through the ups and downs of your work. Sharing your creative energy creates synergy: you'll get more out than you put in.

IF YOU HAVE KNOWLEDGE, LET OTHERS LIGHT
THEIR CANDLES IN IT.

—Margaret Fuller

Feeling competitive rather than collaborative? Meet some of history's great creative rivals on page 55.

If something isn't broken, fix it

Martin and Allyson Egbert set out on a quest to find an alternative treatment for their son. He was born with congenital clubfoot, a rare but crippling deformity. The standard treatment in the late 1990s was years of surgery that left the feet scarred and stiff. Surely there was a better way. The Egberts phoned, surfed the Internet, asked questions and probed.

They discovered an overlooked treatment created in the 1940s by Dr. Ignacio Ponseti. Ponseti had studied the anatomy of the foot and developed a nonsurgical technique that manipulated the baby's feet when they were young and flexible, then held them in place with a plaster cast for a short while. It was highly effective and delivered good results.

Despite the clear advantages of the Ponseti method, and the unequivocal clinical evidence of its effectiveness, it met with opposition. A surgical technique was being transformed into a nonsurgical technique. Surgeons were proud of their skills, and here was someone telling them that surgery was not the best remedy. Ponseti's experience is not unusual for those who produce something groundbreaking: they're surrounded by people who at best are resistant to new ideas, and at worst willfully ignore them.

The Egberts visited the retired Dr. Ponseti to ask him to correct their baby's clubfoot. On their way home, they determined to start a website to explain the technique to other parents. Eventually the Ponseti method gained acceptance and dramatically changed thousands of lives. It took someone outside the medical profession to see the condition clearly, and to find a better solution.

Search for a better method when everyone else is content with the standard. Question tried-and-true techniques. There is always a better way.

ITERATION, LIKE FRICTION, IS LIKELY TO
GENERATE HEAT INSTEAD OF PROGRESS.

— George Eliot

... and if it ain't broke, break it, on page 50.

light a fire in your mind

Contrast the writer James Joyce with his daughter Lucia. Both were troubled people. Joyce wrote all day, every day. He poured his difficulties into his writing, using his art form as a means of self-analysis and repair. He was his own therapist and became an expert on the workings of his own mind. No doctor could diagnose his problems and cure him better than he could. Writing stabilized his life. Creativity enables us to doctor ourselves. Joyce saw that Lucia, on the other hand, was slipping into madness, and he valiantly tried to prevent it. He realized that her dancing career was not enough to save her as writing had saved him. He desperately encouraged Lucia to take up illustration and, when that didn't work, writing. She couldn't find an enthusiasm to engross her as Joyce had, and eventually she was committed to an asylum.

Joyce commented on Lucia inheriting her challenges from him: "Whatever spark or gift I possess has been transmitted to Lucia and it has kindled a fire in the brain." Joyce used the fire in his brain to light up the world of literature. It was a source of inspiration and energy. Lucia's fire had no outlet and burned her up. Joyce saw the opportunity in his difficulties; Lucia saw the difficulty in her opportunities.

Creativity requires us to study the dark corners of our minds and come to terms with what we find. Don't run from your inner demons. Put them to work.

IN THE DEPTHS OF WINTER I FINALLY LEARNED
THERE WAS IN ME AN INVINCIBLE SUMMER.

—Albert Camus

Be positive about negatives on page 21.

discover how to discover

Miuccia Prada kept searching, even though she didn't know what she was looking for. She had lived many different lives before discovering fashion. After graduating with a PhD in political science, she became a member of the Communist Party and a champion of women's rights. Later she studied and performed as a mime artist at venues like La Scala. Eventually these influences were poured into her fashion brand, giving Prada more depth and richer ideals than most fashion houses.

Miuccia Prada was a fashion designer by profession, but she was also an art curator, film producer, fledgling architect, feminist, capitalist and Communist. She proved that a great modern designer could be a mogul, a film producer, a curator, a gallery owner and a lightning rod for other creatives who felt connected to her vision of personal transformation. Most designers emulate trends, but Prada *is* the trend.

Not everyone is born knowing what he or she wants to do. Many have to discover their passion by trial and error. Along the way they discover things that are useful, even though they might not realize it at the time. The media presents many stories of stars who were "born" tennis players or "born" performers; but when you examine their lives more closely, you find it's often the case that their family pushed them into tennis or performing. For most people, discovering what they truly want to do is a long journey, but worth it.

Van Gogh lived for thirty years before he discovered painting. He sensed he had a purpose, but didn't know what it was. When he took up painting seriously, it was the first time he found a satisfying outlet for his nervous energy. Painting gave him a deeper understanding of himself.

Keep searching. Every important experience adjusts our perspective. It's what we do with those experiences that matters.

> I MAY NOT HAVE GONE WHERE I INTENDED TO GO, BUT I THINK I HAVE ENDED UP WHERE I NEEDED TO BE.
>
> —*Douglas Adams*

More? Meet another fashion icon who refused to follow the rules on page 31. Less? Find out who's to blame for the myth of god-given talent on page 8.

to stand out, work out what you stand for

Filippo Marinetti wrote the first art manifesto of the twentieth century. It wasn't cold and logical like a corporation or political party manifesto might be; rather, it conveyed the intense emotion of the futurist movement. It declared futurism to be a rejection of the past and a celebration of speed, violence and youth—the things the futurists cared about most.

Poet Tristan Tzara's 1918 Dada Manifesto is a blistering rant: "DADA DOES NOT MEAN ANYTHING." André Breton's 1924 *Le Manifeste du Surréalisme* begins, "We are still living under the reign of logic." The designer John Maeda's manifesto proclaims, "More emotions are better than less." The writer Leo Tolstoy decreed, "Change nothing in your style of living even if you become ten times richer." And in their joint manifesto, painters Mark Rothko, Adolph Gottlieb and Barnett Newman declared, "This world of imagination is fancy-free and violently opposed to common sense."

Developing a set of principles you believe in and constantly strive to uphold is an invaluable tool. Manifestos are traditionally public declarations, but anyone can have a personal manifesto. Don't make it a dreary list of worthy intentions drenched in morality. It's a medium through which your present self can correspond with your future self. The only way to stand out is to work out what you stand for. Write it down for yourself so you can live it out loud.

MAN OFTEN BECOMES WHAT HE BELIEVES
HIMSELF TO BE.

—*Mahatma Gandhi*

Meet the conservative revolutionaries who knew better than anyone what they stood for on page 91.

to achieve something, do nothing

The great crime writer Raymond Chandler set aside at least four hours each day to do nothing. He explained his two simple rules for this time: "A. You don't have to write. B. You can't do anything else. The rest comes of itself." He didn't force himself to write, but he stopped himself from doing anything else. No reading, writing letters, tidying—nothing. Without distractions, his imagination wandered and he'd think up a story. He almost always ended up writing for the full four hours.

Creativity is the most difficult thing the human mind has to tackle. Tidying, cleaning, organizing, answering emails, cruising the Internet, doing research, reformatting a document, planning meetings, attending meetings, arranging pre-meeting meetings . . . Every other chore seems easier and therefore more alluring.

Do you want a tidy home and a blank canvas, or a messy home and a completed canvas? (Writing this book has caused me to be two years behind on my ironing.) We find it hard to pause, or just be still, in our 24/7 culture. Look at people waiting in line and you'll see they immediately take out their phones and check their emails and texts. Our hyperactive culture believes it is better to be doing something, even if it's futile or worthless, than doing nothing.

Many writers prefer to write in cafés—J.K. Rowling famously remarked that "This got me away from the temptations of the Internet. At home, by contrast, there's no end to the useful tasks that I can find to occupy myself."

Make yourself do nothing. Let your thoughts settle. Sometimes we need to be patient. Instead of searching, let things come to you. The ideas and solutions are within us, but we are occupied with mundane matters. We are looking in the wrong direction.

Sometimes what we most need to do is the thing we most try to avoid. If you want to do something creative, something original, do nothing.

IT IS THE JOB THAT IS NEVER STARTED THAT TAKES LONGEST TO FINISH.

—*J.R.R. Tolkien*

Inspired? Try working the hours that work for you, and no more on page 93—or achieve the perfect work-life balance on page 147.

get into credit

There was an extraordinary outburst of creativity in Florence during the early 1400s. Great artists sprang up like wildflowers. Donatello, Ghiberti and Masaccio created a huge number of history's greatest masterpieces. Was it caused by a freak mutation in the gene pool?

No, it was money. Florence was the richest city in Europe due to trading and manufacture. There were a dozen major bankers, including the Medicis, earning fortunes in interest from money lent to foreign countries. The Medicis spent astronomical sums of money on the architects and artists who built and decorated Florence. Artists flocked to Florence like bees to a honeypot. The seeds of the Renaissance were planted and bloomed, creating civilization as we know it.

Creativity flourishes where there is money. Money is not the enemy of creative thinkers but the friend; not a problem but an opportunity. The creative mind needs to focus on creativity; financial worries are at best a distraction and at worst a crippling weight. Research shows that the size of Van Gogh's canvases fluctuated in proportion to his finances. Lack of money literally shrank his paintings. More than five thousand American artists and writers, among them Mark Rothko, Jackson Pollock, Ben Shahn and Jack Kerouac, benefitted from the American government pouring money into the Works Progress Administration—a project to promote American culture after World War II. Artists, writers and musicians were financed for two years, which gave them the time and space to develop, to find their voices. The flowering of Young British Artists in London in the 1980s was largely due to Charles Saatchi's generous development of his art collection—in turn financed by the boom in advertising revenues. Holland was the richest nation in seventeenth-century Europe and saw the golden age of Dutch painting, with Frans Hals, Vermeer, Jan Steen and Rembrandt. The history of art is inseparable from the history of money.

Artists are often coy about discussing money, but there's no doubt it can be a great facilitator—and, in its absence, a massive distraction. Being clear about the role of finances clears the way to doing more of what you love.

MONEY IS BETTER THAN POVERTY, IF ONLY FOR FINANCIAL REASONS.

—*Woody Allen*

Feeling the pinch? Learn how to prosper in a recession on page 181.

Search high and low

I thought I saw someone vandalizing a Jeff Koons sculpture. It was late evening in New York. He moved with jerky, manic and intense gestures. I should have known better, but I couldn't stop myself, I was compelled to intervene.

The Koons sculpture was *Puppy*, a giant West Highland terrier made of flowers. Koons stated that this cloying, gaudy monster was a symbol of "love, warmth and happiness." It towered forty feet above me. Twenty-three tons of soil covered a steel structure swathed in seventy thousand red, orange, white and pink flowering petunias, begonias and chrysanthemums. It was midway through construction and the workers had left the site unattended. As I got closer, I could see the vandal's darting, frenzied eyes as he moved the plants around with agitated gestures.

Puppy was a distillation of American culture: big, bright, colorful, popular—and seriously crazy. Art aficionados spent hours pondering its meaning; others simply laughed and enjoyed it. Unlike much contemporary art, it reached out to viewers and they responded. Koons uses kitsch and vulgar sculptures to challenge the accepted aesthetic taste of the "highbrow." He constantly stretches and amplifies tasteless trash and rubs the noses of exclusive art-world patrons in it. The huge scale of his sculptures makes them unavoidable. He has put gaudy kitsch in the most rarified museums on the planet. *Puppy* now stands permanently outside the Guggenheim Museum in Bilbao.

The crazy vandal, by the way, of course turned out to be Jeff Koons. A perfectionist, he was working late, attending to details. He was friendly and warm and asked if I'd like to place a few flowers.

Creative thinkers like Koons mock the idea of "high" and "low" culture, "good" and "bad." They don't consider an episode of *The Simpsons* to be better or worse than a Shakespeare play. Each has qualities. They see no incompatibility between being tuned in to Jay Z one minute and Mahler the next. If we dismiss "low" culture, we are missing out on a huge area of life.

The terms "highbrow" and "lowbrow" come from the populist science of phrenology that boomed in the late nineteenth century. The shape of the skull was used to identify intelligence. A high forehead signified intelligence; a low one meant stupidity. Real science has completely discredited phrenology, but its ideas linger on. You can't think creatively if you have elitist attitudes. Snobbery is a straitjacket.

In 1982 Craig Good was not valued by society. He'd done a variety of jobs and was currently unemployed. He applied for a janitorial and security job at Pixar, which at the time was still a department within Lucasfilm. Scrubbing toilets was the main task. "If you want to learn a lot about a company," Good said, "being a janitor is a pretty good way to do it." Pixar offered an after-work programming course, open to all employees. Good attended, and was soon moved to the company's computer division. He eventually became a camera artist at Pixar, a role he played for thirty years. He is famous for his work on *Toy Story*, *Finding Nemo* and *Monsters, Inc.* Good's career is proof that Pixar values all employees for their potential, no matter what their position.

"One of the characteristics that made Pixar, and is very rare and important, is that the corporate culture recognized that contributions can come from everybody, anybody," Pam Kerwin, Pixar's vice president, has said. Pixar screens each film numerous times for everyone in the company while it is in production, and invites anyone to make suggestions.

Creative thinkers put aside the value judgments that affect the rest of society. They don't assume that because everyone thinks something is worthless, it actually is. They are able to see things clearly and assess them according to their own values.

OUR ATTITUDES CONTROL OUR LIVES.
ATTITUDES ARE A SECRET POWER WORKING
TWENTY-FOUR HOURS A DAY, FOR GOOD OR BAD.
IT IS OF PARAMOUNT IMPORTANCE THAT WE
KNOW HOW TO HARNESS AND CONTROL THIS
GREAT FORCE.

—*Irving Berlin*

Inspired to suspend judgment? Listen for the sweetest sound of all on page 105.

mine your mind

Many entrepreneurs' best ideas have come to them in their dreams. Elias Howe is credited with inventing the modern sewing machine, which has been remarkably successful due to its innovation of putting the eye of the needle at the point.

Howe's family members explained how he came up with the idea. In his first attempts he put the eye of the needle at the conventional end, but it didn't work. Then one night he had a dream in which he was ordered to build a sewing machine by a cruel king in a strange country. The king gave him twenty-four hours or he'd be executed. He struggled with the needle's eye, but just as in real life, he couldn't make it work. He was taken out to be executed and noticed that the soldiers had spears that were pierced near the point. The solution presented itself. The inventor begged for more time. At that point he woke up. It was four in the morning. He jumped out of bed, ran to his workshop and created a needle with an eye at the point.

The subconscious is a recognized source of creativity and inspiration; it releases us from the confines of our logical, practical mind. When our conscious mind is switched off—because we are driving, taking a shower, scrubbing the floor, or asleep and dreaming—ideas bubble up to the surface. When we are not trying to think, the door to the cage opens and our minds fly off in unpredictable directions and often land on the solution. Salvador Dalí had dreamed about a hand with hundreds of ants crawling over it. The film director Luis Buñuel dreamed of a cloud cutting through the moon like a razor blade slicing through an eye. They put the two together in a film called *Un Chien Andalou* and created one of cinema's most memorable moments. Richard Wagner dreamed the prelude to *Das Rheingold*. Lewis Carroll's *Alice's Adventures in Wonderland* is a journey into his subconscious.

The creative ideas you're searching for are swimming beneath the surface of your mind. The deeper you dive, the more you'll discover.

THE WORLD NEEDS DREAMERS AND THE WORLD
NEEDS DOERS. BUT ABOVE ALL, THE WORLD
NEEDS DREAMERS WHO DO.

— *Sarah Ban Breathnach*

Feeling dreamy? Follow Hans Christian Andersen and go out of your mind on page 176. Already had your good idea? Bring it to life on page 71.

look forward to disappointment

When Beethoven was young, he struggled to earn a living as a musician, to get married and lead a normal life. When he finally achieved success, in his late twenties, he began to lose his hearing. It was his lowest point. He sank into a deep depression. In a letter he declared, "The most beautiful years of my life must pass without accomplishing the promise of my talent and powers." Six months later, Beethoven decided, "No! I cannot endure it. I will take Fate by the throat; it shall not wholly overcome me." Thus began his rise to the summit of his achievements.

Beethoven transformed his obstacle into a positive force. His music conveys this self-reflection and self-awareness; he used his compositions to come to a greater understanding of himself. Beethoven's music was a healing force for himself, and so in turn it helps us heal our wounds.

When you are at your lowest, when everything that could go wrong has gone wrong, see it as the best place to begin. We learn more from disappointments than from successes. Every obstacle we overcome strengthens our confidence to overcome more. Beethoven overcame the seemingly insurmountable obstacle of deafness. Creative people always have their ideas, ambitions, passions and memories to support them.

ALL MISFORTUNE IS BUT A STEPPING STONE TO
FORTUNE.

—*Henry David Thoreau*

Feeling similarly restricted? Turn it to your advantage on page 186.

Feeling similarly restricted? Turn it to your advantage on page 186.

think with your feelings

The teacher handed out toothpicks and semi-dried peas and asked the class to make model buildings. The children formed cubes because that's what they were used to seeing in the streets. A boy with severely bad eyesight, however, had only touch to rely on and discovered that the triangle (or tetrahedron) felt far more solid and stable than fragile squares. He quickly constructed complicated latticeworks. Due to the triangle's strength as a shape, his structures were much bigger and more elegant than his classmates'. The teacher was astonished and called the other children over to see the unique construction. The boy was surprised at their surprise—it had seemed natural to him. His bad eyesight prevented him from seeing the boxlike lines of the houses, windows and door frames we are all surrounded by, so he had used touch, and achieved better results.

Two decades later, the boy, Buckminster Fuller, had become a groundbreaking architect, and his childhood structure, the geodesic dome, was recognized as an ingenious and economical way to build strong, large structures with no need for internal support. There are now hundreds of thousands of the domes all over the world.

We are taught how to think and what to think, but any creative person will tell you that thinking only gets you so far. Thinking is essential, but we use it to the detriment of other perceptions.

Our minds play tricks on us, but our senses are trustworthy. We have been taught to choose the respectable, socially acceptable and well-trodden path that everyone else walks down. Instead, choose the path that feels right to you.

BETTER TO BE WITHOUT LOGIC THAN WITHOUT FEELING.

— *Charlotte Brontë*

Still overthinking? Try contradicting yourself for once on page 193.

bring chaos to order

The Guggenheim Museum in Bilbao, Spain, is full of surprises. The outside walls are a surprise—they're cloaked in titanium tiles that create a weightless and iridescent feel. Inside, the complex shapes that whirl above the soaring, 150-foot-high atrium are a revelation. To the side, light is diffused through glass slashes in the teetering walls, casting perpetually changing, astonishing shadows. The building is like a car crash—and that is meant as a compliment. The distorted and dislocated areas create dynamic and unexpected clashes. Metal crashes into stone, man-made smashes into natural, and flowing forms slice into rigid angular forms. The building is a great testament to the benefits of chaos over order. Simply walking through it is exciting and energizing.

Frank Gehry is one of architecture's great visionaries. Inventive and irreverent, his twisted forms break the conventions of building design and always stir up controversy. Much of his work falls within the style of deconstructivism, characterized by unpredictability, chaos and fragmentation. The Guggenheim was an audacious design that shook architecture to its core when it opened in 1997. Its immediate success catapulted the formerly unknown Spanish city onto the world stage.

The success of the Guggenheim was due to Gehry's unique design—and his unique creative process. Instead of the usual extensive blueprints, the contractors hired to build the Guggenheim were simply given Gehry's small model, and were challenged to work out the measurements themselves. This resulted in inaccuracies—which Gehry liked—along with the invention of new construction techniques, and a physical environment filled with chaotic twists and turns that keep you continually surprised and delighted. From chaos springs great art.

What's true of a Spanish architectural masterpiece is also true of our workplace. It flies in the face of conventional wisdom, but a chaotic office or studio is more productive. Chaotic organizations are usually more creative than well-organized ones. Resist the idea that we should strive for order over all else. Play with chaos and see what happens.

IF A CLUTTERED DESK IS A SIGN OF A
CLUTTERED MIND, OF WHAT, THEN, IS AN
EMPTY DESK A SIGN?

—*Albert Einstein*

Inspired? Try improvising your way out of a problem on page 6. Uninspired? Meet a slightly more methodical (but still subversive) creative on page 164.

take what you need

A student at Stanford University discovered the short stories of John Cheever. He decided to type them out word for word, page for page. He stepped into Cheever's shoes and felt what it was like to have "written" the stories. Rather like da Vinci dissecting a heart to try to understand how it worked, the student was trying to get inside Cheever's mind. He went on to become the prolific fiction writer Ethan Canin; there have been four Hollywood films based on his stories. "It's interesting because you learn things," Canin explained. "Something simple about Cheever is that his paragraphs are much longer than yours would have been. His sentences are longer. He pushes everything further than I would have pushed them." From that "pushing further" Canin learned to be more extreme in his writing. He learned from Cheever's technique, then he learned from Cheever's thought process. Canin didn't copy him slavishly, though. Humans are not photocopy machines. Where he failed to emulate Cheever accurately was where he began to be original. It was this difference he magnified. You can borrow flour, but you have to bake your own bread.

Copying as an exercise is not the same as plagiarism. Plagiarism would be if you signed a painting someone else had done, or otherwise pretended you had done someone else's work. Everyone has influences. One of the reasons that great artists cluster together geographically is so that they can learn from one another. Jacques Lipchitz explains, "I remember one day when Juan Gris told me about a bunch of grapes he had seen in a painting by Picasso. The next day these grapes appeared in a painting by Gris, this time in a bowl; and the day after, the bowl appeared in a painting by Picasso."

Copying is often misunderstood by people who are not creative. A lot of our behavior comes from observing and emulating others, not least fundamental abilities like walking and talking. Later, we practice what the psychologist Albert Bandura refers to as "modeling." We are more likely to smoke if our friends smoke, more likely to overeat if our friends overeat. You emulate the people around you. So choose carefully which creative thinkers you surround yourself with.

Rembrandt was an apprentice before he went on to produce original paintings. He learned from the masters, but then his unique vision emerged. When you see a piece of work you admire, dissect it dispassionately and discover exactly what makes it great. Is it the style? The concept? The creator's personality? Embrace good ideas and techniques wherever you can find them—and then make them your own.

CHANCE FAVORS THE CONNECTED MIND.

—*Steven Johnson*

Hungry to cross-pollinate? Try page 164. Prefer to strive for something completely original? Surprise yourself with your own story on page 102.

remake, then remake the remake

The composer and lyricist Stephen Sondheim had a flop on his hands. When the Broadway production of his musical *Merrily We Roll Along* opened, the critics savaged it and it ran for only sixteen performances. Audiences were confused and couldn't follow the story. It was a shock for Sondheim; he has written many great musicals, including *West Side Story*, won an Academy Award and three Grammy nominations; you name a theater award and he's won it. So how did he deal with a flop?

Sondheim reworked *Merrily We Roll Along*, again and again. Over the years the musical has been restaged with numerous songs discarded and replaced with new versions. Each time it was performed the composer revised it by adding a new song. Sondheim believed in the musical; he was sure of his ability, sure of his original idea, but he was also able to question and to deconstruct the parts that didn't work for audiences. Eventually it showed in London and then back on Broadway to ecstatic reviews, decades after its first, disastrous appearance.

The first spark of inspiration often requires revision. Ernest Hemingway explained, "I wrote the ending to *Farewell to Arms*, the last page of it, thirty-nine times before I was satisfied." That means he discarded thirty-eight endings. He constantly took an axe to his work and rebuilt it. The creative enjoy the revision process—carving away excess words, clay or notes until the rhythm and phrasing and shape of their work purrs like a well-tuned engine. Many ask for help with their revision process. T. S. Eliot enlisted Ezra Pound to give him extensive feedback on his most important poem, *The Waste Land*. In the original manuscript Pound scribbled numerous comments such as "verse not interesting enough." Without Pound's help it would never have become a classic.

When a printing deadline approached, J.R.R. Tolkien, author of *The Lord of the Rings*, intensively revised, reconsidered and polished his manuscript. Tolkien rewrote so thoroughly that many new ideas sprang from him, and the publisher, expecting a completed text, instead often received the first draft of a completely new work. D. H. Lawrence rewrote *Lady Chatterley's Lover* from start to finish three times before it was ready to publish. Similarly, Picasso's greatest masterpiece, the huge oil painting *Guernica*, has been presented as a bolt from the blue, a flash of inspiration. The myth is that Picasso heard of the bombing of the small town of Guernica during World War II and painted an instinctive response: a visual account of the devastating and chaotic impact of war on both men and women, specifically on civilian life and communities. What is less well known is that Picasso produced forty-five preliminary sketches for *Guernica* before he even began painting. Archive photos of the painting in progress reveal numerous layers of adjustments and radical changes; the final product took weeks to paint.

Let go of the image of art as instant masterpiece. Instead, be prepared to constantly rethink and revise.

YOU MIGHT NOT WRITE WELL EVERY DAY, BUT YOU CAN ALWAYS EDIT A BAD PAGE. YOU CAN'T EDIT A BLANK PAGE.

—*Jodi Picoult*

More? Meet a quartet that exemplifies the merits of working hard to make it look easy on page 151. Less? Cut it out on page 45.

be curious about curiosity

Eric Blair deliberately got himself arrested so that he could spend Christmas in prison. He was curious to see what it would be like. Unfortunately the authorities didn't consider his disorderly behavior serious enough and released him. Blair was fascinated by how people at the opposite end of the social spectrum lived. He was born into an elite, wealthy, upper-class family and educated at Eton. Suddenly he began dressing in ragged clothes and shoes and living rough with the homeless on the streets of London and Paris. Reading about poverty was not enough for him; he wanted to experience it for himself. He didn't carry spare money for emergencies or wear layers of clothes for protection against the freezing conditions. He wanted the authentic feel of hunger, cold and hopelessness.

Blair's experiences were recorded in the book *Down and Out in Paris and London*, vivid accounts of the places and characters he found living on the margins. He exposed extraordinary life stories as well as the resourcefulness and resilience of people discarded by society. He challenged his prejudices, cultivated his curiosity and discovered years' worth of inspiration for writing and novels. He changed his name to George Orwell so that his parents and friends wouldn't be embarrassed by his exploits, and went on to write some of the twentieth century's classic novels, including *1984* and *Animal Farm*.

The future belongs to the curious. Curiosity makes us come alive; it fills us with wonder and the urge to discover hidden worlds. Curiosity is the engine of achievement. It's what drives us to keep questioning, keep discovering and continuing to break new ground. As Einstein famously said, "I have no special talents. I am only passionately curious."

Curious people search for the reality behind the façade, for what's truly going on behind the scenes. They ask difficult questions. Albert Einstein explained further, "The important thing is not to stop questioning. Curiosity has its own reason for existing. One cannot help but be in awe when he contemplates the mysteries of eternity, of life, of the marvelous structure of reality. It is enough if one tries merely to comprehend a little of this mystery every day." Cultivate your curiosity and you will constantly refresh your perspective.

THE CURE FOR BOREDOM IS CURIOSITY. THERE IS NO CURE FOR CURIOSITY.

—*Dorothy Parker*

Curiosity not sated? Try projecting yourself into the future on page 182.

become anonymous

When J.K. Rowling had become the world's highest-selling author, she stunned the book world by revealing that *The Cuckoo's Calling* was her work, written under the pseudonym Robert Galbraith. Rowling said, "I had hoped to keep this secret a little longer, because being Robert Galbraith has been such a liberating experience." Agatha Christie wrote sixty-six successful detective novels under her own name. She also wrote six romance novels under the name Mary Westmacott. Christie wanted to explore another genre without the baggage of her reputation weighing her down. Many novelists want to experiment with new genres. John Banville achieved recognition as a serious writer by winning the Man Booker Prize in 2005, but he also writes crime novels as Benjamin Black. Julian Barnes, another Man Booker–winning author, writes thrillers as Dan Kavanagh. A pseudonym gave them all the freedom to write without the shackles of their reputations, and an opportunity to explore genres that are not generally taken seriously.

Robert Towne is a legendary Hollywood scriptwriter. He worked behind the scenes on classics such as *Bonnie and Clyde* and *The Godfather*, for which he didn't demand any credit. He mentored Jeremy Larner, who won an Oscar for writing *The Candidate*. "I couldn't have written it without him," said Larner. Sometimes Towne was hired to write a script for which he knew he'd get the credit; and then weeks and months would go by without a script materializing. If Towne was working anonymously, he worked freely and quickly. If he knew he was going to get the credit for a script, he suffered from writer's block. He kept rewriting and rewriting, but the script didn't ever reach a conclusion. Eventually he would be given a deadline. He wouldn't keep to it and was often dropped from the project. After working for years on a film called *Greystoke: The Legend of Tarzan, Lord of the Apes*, Towne became disillusioned and gave the credit for the script to his dog, P.H. Vazak. Vazak was the first dog (and I suspect the last) nominated for an Academy Award for screenwriting.

Sometimes it's useful to put your ego in a box under the bed. There is freedom in being nobody. Working under another name will free you of others' expectations and, most importantly, free you of your own.

IT'S THAT ANONYMOUS PERSON WHO MEANDERS THROUGH THE STREETS AND FEELS WHAT'S HAPPENING THERE, FEELS THE PULSE OF THE PEOPLE, WHO'S ABLE TO CREATE.

— *Cyndi Lauper*

Ego still bothering you? Get out of yourself on page 178, or remind yourself of the pleasures of obscurity on page 113.

achieve the perfect work-life balance

The way to achieve the perfect work-life balance is simple: don't do any work. If your work and life are in separate compartments, something's gone wrong. Great painters, poets, dancers, artists, entrepreneurs and other creative people choose a lifestyle and then work out what they have to do to make a living within that way of life. They choose an authentic and fulfilling life rather than fulfilling society's expectations. Most of all, they get to do what they love, 24-7.

Hunter S. Thompson, spokesman for the Beat Generation, wanted to spend his life writing, so he set about earning his living through journalism and writing novels such as *Fear and Loathing in Las Vegas*. Thompson was never rich, but he lived the lifestyle that suited him. He fulfilled his potential as a writer. A ceremony was held for him after he died in which his ashes were fired from a cannon. He literally went out with a bang.

Thompson jotted down this advice to a friend: "As I see it then, the formula runs something like this: a man must choose a path that will let his abilities function at maximum efficiency toward the gratification of his desires." Thompson continues, "In short, he has not dedicated his life to reaching a predefined goal, but he has rather chosen a way of life he knows he will enjoy." Thompson achieved these ambitions. He sometimes had to scratch out a living through journalism, but he was writing what he believed and that was what mattered most.

The creative person's work and life are one, inseparable. Their life *is* their work. There is no "balance" because they are bound together. Once your life and work head down separate paths you are destined for a disconnected existence. If you'd rather go on vacation than go to work—you need to change your life, now.

> IF YOU'RE INTERESTED IN "BALANCING" WORK
> AND PLEASURE, STOP TRYING TO BALANCE
> THEM. INSTEAD MAKE YOUR WORK MORE
> PLEASURABLE.
>
> —*Donald Trump*

Inspired? Try changing your body clock at the same time on page 93.

make what you say unforgettable

The celebrated physiologist Giles Brindley found an original way to convey his ideas. The audience will never forget his lecture at the American Urological Association meeting in Las Vegas in 1983. The *New York Times* declared Brindley's spectacle the start of a "second sexual revolution." Not bad for a pre-dinner talk at a medical convention, to an audience of rather pompous doctors dressed in formal attire.

Brindley explained his theory to the assembled group: that it was possible to inject chemicals into the penis to cause an erection. At the time very little was known about erectile physiology. Viagra and the days when politicians and soccer legends spoke candidly about their struggles with erectile dysfunction were still years away.

In the absence of suitable animal models, Brindley had experimented on himself. He showed images of his own penis in various states of tumescence—much to the audience's surprise. He explained that it was such an effective method that a single dose made an impotent man stay hard for hours.

Brindley was concerned that skeptics might question whether erotic stimulation had played a part in achieving the results. The professor wanted to make his case in the most convincing way possible, so he had injected himself shortly before the talk. He pointed out that no one would find the experience of giving a lecture to a large audience erotically stimulating, then dropped his trousers to reveal his clearly erect penis. There was not a sound in the room. Everyone had stopped breathing. Brindley then said, "I'd like to give some of the audience the opportunity to confirm the degree of tumescence." He shuffled to the first row of the horrified audience. Women seated at the first few tables threw their arms up and screamed loudly. The screams seemed to shock Professor Brindley (who later received a knighthood for his bioengineering research), and he rapidly pulled up his trousers, returned to the podium and ended the lecture. The crowd dispersed in a state of stunned silence.

The impact of Brindley's presentation changed the course of men's health forever. More importantly, he'd found a creative way to make an impact on the medical world.

An original thinker is a scout on new horizons, a font of inspiration. He or she finds a way to communicate an idea that makes it impossible to forget. Original thinkers are creative in the way they get their message across. If you have an interesting idea, it's important that people remember it. The people who have changed our thinking are the ones who speak and write from the heart, with the courage to simply be who they are. Summon the courage to head toward a new frontier without a map.

ONCE SOMETHING IS MEMORABLE, IT'S LIVING AND YOU'RE USING IT. THAT TO ME IS THE FOUNDATION OF A CREATIVE SOCIETY.

— *Yo-Yo Ma*

More? Learn how to be as annoying as Jonathan Swift on page 174. Less? See the downside of nudity during public speaking on page 38.

don't experiment,
be an experiment

The Beatles became the most influential cultural force of their era by following a principle: constant experimentation. They searched for new methods to make music, consistently explored new musical territory with each album, and when they described how they worked in the recording studio, it sounded more like a sound laboratory. More fundamentally, they continually reinvented their music by injecting it with fresh influences. Paul McCartney explained their recording philosophy: "We would say, 'Try it. Just try it for us. If it sounds crappy, OK, we'll lose it. But it might just sound good.' We were always pushing ahead: louder, further, longer, more, different." They experimented with mixing several genres together. They were the first rock band to use feedback (on "I Feel Fine"), the sitar and Indian music (on *Revolver*), a string quartet (on "Yesterday"). The Beatles loved technology: they used artificial double tracking, close miking of acoustic instruments, sampling, direct injection, synchronizing tape machines and playing tapes backward. All these experiments added the multiple dimensions to their work that make it so deeply layered.

Lennon and McCartney constantly played around with ways to improve each other's songs. Occasionally they would combine two incomplete songs that each had produced individually to create a complete song ("A Day in the Life," for example). Sometimes one of the two added a middle eight to the other's verse and chorus. Lennon called it "writing eyeball-to-eyeball." It created an atmosphere where they felt free to add all kinds of experimental ideas to each other's music. When you listen to tapes of them in the studio, you hear that they are always adding jokes, outrageous lyrics and strange sounds to each other's work.

The key to thinking experimentally is to allow the mind to contemplate outrageous ideas. This requires enormous effort. We are taught to dismiss novel and seemingly ridiculous ideas at the outset, and to think logically. Strive to lose that impulse and return to the creative freedom we all had as children. It's more interesting to be experimental and fail than to play it safe and succeed.

When I was a student at the Royal College of Art, the student working next to me found an old painting on a scrap of paper at the back of a drawer. He liked parts of it, so he cut it up into pieces and recombined them in a new arrangement that was much more interesting than the original. I looked closely at it. I could see fragments of writing scattered across the composition. I pointed out that the fragments were the signature of a previous student, "David Hockney." I have never seen anyone turn so pale. The student had transformed an old painting into something better, but reduced its value from tens of thousands of dollars to nothing. The moral of the story? Sometimes there's a downside to experimentation: not all experiments are successful. To get into the experimental mindset, you have to accept that there will be many fruitless attempts, even disasters. There is no way of knowing what will work and what won't, but every failed experiment will teach you something new.

We are all confronted by problems, but an experimental approach can lead to unique and original solutions. Creative thinkers use their office, studio or workplace as a place to experiment, a laboratory. Creative organizations practice constant experimentation to keep their thinking fresh.

If things are running too smoothly, it's a sign that you're not experimenting enough.

I HAVE ALWAYS BEEN MORE INTERESTED IN
EXPERIMENT THAN IN ACCOMPLISHMENT.

— *Orson Welles*

Agree? Find something that's working and break it on page 50. Disagree? Find something that doesn't need improving and improve it on page 117.

Stop missing opportunities

How many opportunities have you missed? I've lost count of the number of people I know who have been given one and didn't take it. They were blasé. They assumed another would come along, then another and another. But they didn't. These people had one chance, and they let it pass them by. In retrospect, they bitterly regret it. Opportunities are often rare and fleeting.

The great Hollywood actor, director and producer Warren Beatty was nominated for fourteen Academy Awards during his career, and once won the Best Director award. His most famous acting role was as Clyde Barrow in *Bonnie and Clyde*. In 1964 he wanted to put together a film he could star in. His idea became *What's New Pussycat?* It was a comedy about a notorious womanizer who wanted to be faithful to his girlfriend but was continually tempted by women who kept falling in love with him.

Beatty found a producer and they set to work on the script. They soon realized they needed someone to write good jokes. At a club in New York called the Bitter End they saw a young comic called Woody Allen doing stand-up. He was funny, so they offered him $30,000 a week to add a few jokes to the script. Allen tried to get $40,000 a week. "No" was the response. Allen said he'd do it for $30,000 if he could also have a small cameo role. They agreed.

Allen went to work. As draft followed draft, Beatty noticed that his role was getting slighter as the unknown Allen's got bigger. Allen continued to expand his character as Beatty's shrank smaller and smaller. Eventually Beatty angrily stormed away from the project. *What's New Pussycat?* went on to be a big success. From that moment on, Allen was a significant Hollywood A-lister and made sure he was always in total control of his work. He made the most of his opportunity. He might never have got another one. It was a small opportunity but he made it big.

I've known many artists who were offered a one-person exhibition—their big chance!—but argued with the gallery owner about some small contractual detail and the deal fell through. They were never offered another exhibition. I've known writers who wanted a slightly bigger advance than the publisher was offering. They rejected their big break.

When you're given an opportunity, take it and see where it leads, even if you have no idea how you'll make it work. Say yes, then work out how to pull it off. Rise to the occasion when an occasion arises.

> ONE SECRET OF SUCCESS IN LIFE IS FOR A MAN
> TO BE READY FOR HIS OPPORTUNITY WHEN IT
> COMES.
>
> —*Benjamin Disraeli*

Can't see any opportunities worth taking? Create your own on page 20, or hold out for a recession on page 181.

Contradict yourself more often

Eminent psychologist Mihaly Csikszentmihalyi has observed that creative people "contain contradictory extremes; instead of being an individual, each of them is a multitude."

The English painter Francis Bacon was a fascinating example of how conflicting personality traits are essential to produce great art. Bacon was a giant of twentieth-century art who captured the anxieties and frenetic energy of the century with brutality and tenderness. His violent paintings are revered and hated in equal measure.

In many ways Bacon's paintings are indecisive. They are portraits, but the people in them are often unrecognizable. They lurch from abstract areas to figurative passages. They are often titled "studies" because Bacon was unable to decide whether or not they were finished.

Psychologists use extroversion and introversion as the most stable personality traits with which to measure people. They can't do this with creative individuals because they exhibit both traits simultaneously, tending to be both extroverted and introverted, sometimes the center of attention, sometimes observers on the fringes. Again, Bacon exemplified this paradox. He frequented the Colony Room, a private members' drinking club in London's Soho that was a magnet for the capital's aspiring creatives. Out with friends, I sometimes found myself in that glorious hellhole. Bacon was usually center stage, in the thick of the party, but only after he'd spent countless long, solitary hours in his studio. He frequently switched from extroversion to introversion.

Bacon exhibited another classic contradiction of creative thinkers: he was simultaneously rebellious and conservative. He was deeply immersed in the traditions and history of painting; he used oil on canvas, painted mainly portraits and placed his paintings in large gold frames. Yet he challenged traditions. He painted on the "wrong," unprimed side of the canvas, he applied the paint with garbage can lids and rags rather than brushes, and his subject matter was shocking and outrageous.

Bacon's paintings reflect the contradictions of his mind. He painted savagely gashed human flesh—with sensitivity. A painstakingly worked area of paint was then attacked by a wildly thrown splash. His brushwork was brutal yet tender. Most of his works contain an area of jet-black against pure white. These contrasts create tension and excitement. It's the contradictions within his mind, and therefore within the paintings, that make them great art.

Although they can be perplexing and frustrating to others, contradictions are an inextricable element of creativity. There is pressure in our culture to be clear what you stand for, to make a decision and stick to it. It's practically a criminal offense to change your mind. The result is rigid thinking. This is true for organizations too. The creative mind contains multiple perspectives simultaneously. Contradicting yourself is a sign that you are brimming with possibilities.

> **ONLY IDIOTS FAIL TO CONTRADICT THEMSELVES THREE TIMES A DAY.**
>
> —*Friedrich Nietzsche*

Perfectionist? Plan to have more accidents on page 82. Lots to do? Pause for thoughtlessness on page 80.

look over the horizon

Some creative people are visionaries. Is it innate or a technique? "It helps to see over the horizon," said entrepreneur Ted Turner. Most people are too preoccupied with the present to look far ahead.

Why is Ted Turner regarded as a visionary entrepreneur? In the seventies Turner could see that the traditional nine-to-five workday was obsolete. Working hours were becoming more flexible. This was at odds with TV schedules; TV stations rigidly timetabled their news programs for 6 and 10 p.m. Turner's idea was a twenty-four-hour news channel that anyone could dip into at any time. CNN covered worldwide news as it unfolded. Unlike the highly edited and smoothly presented mainstream channels, CNN was live, raw and immediate. Events like Poland's Solidarity strike, China's Tiananmen Square uprising, and the 1991 Gulf War were covered live, around the clock. The reporters were breathless and unscripted. Ted Turner revolutionized news reporting and played a big role in the creation of the "global village." CNN became the world's most widely and internationally distributed news channel.

After his father's suicide in 1963, Turner took over the small family billboard business, saved it from bankruptcy and turned it around. Turner applied his visionary process to billboard advertising, the restaurant business, television, and professional sports. He looked into their futures and then brought them into the present—each time creating multimillion-dollar businesses that enabled him to give more than a billion dollars to charity.

Keith Haring was a visionary artist, whose imagery is an instantly recognizable visual language of the twentieth century. At the School of Visual Arts in New York in the 1980s he studied drawing, painting, sculpture and art history. He developed a fluid use of line. His distinctive style was based on bold, graphic icons such as hearts, hands and a "radiant baby" that were often merged with abstract patterns to create richly packed compositions.

Haring looked out for the seeds of the next important art movement, which had always emerged in the downtown galleries before moving uptown. He worked as an assistant in the

Tony Shafrazi Gallery and gained an inside knowledge of the newest trends. The downtown galleries started to exhibit the graffiti artists who were blossoming on the streets and subway, but the work was formulaic—gaudy, multicolored lettering. Every graffiti artist had the same style. Haring saw his chance. He aligned himself with the movement, but his hard-edged black line and use of symbolic imagery stood out. He had a solo exhibition at the gallery and soon afterward stepped into art history.

Visionaries try to work out what the upcoming developments in their field are likely to be and implement them before anyone else. Most people are too busy coping with day-to-day events to lift their heads up and look over the horizon.

A VISIONARY IS SOMEONE WHO CAN SEE THE FUTURE, OR THINKS HE SEES THE FUTURE. IN MY CASE, I USE IT AND IT COMES OUT RIGHT. THAT DOESN'T COME FROM DAYDREAMS OR DREAMS, BUT IT COMES FROM KNOWING THE MARKET AND KNOWING THE WORLD AND KNOWING PEOPLE REALLY WELL AND KNOWING WHERE THEY'RE GOING TO BE TOMORROW.

—*Leonard Lauder*

Yes? Look into the future on page 182. No? Live in the here and now on page 73.

Immerse yourself

Standing next to a film director on a movie set, it's hard to imagine a more stressful job. There's a constant stream of people asking, "How should I light this?" or "How should I say this line?" or "Close-up or long shot?" The director gives precise feedback to the cast and crew of grips, cameramen, lighting engineers, actors, production designers, makeup artists . . . all the time staying within budget. They start at 7 a.m. and usually put in a twenty-hour day, in an atmosphere of total pandemonium. Add to that the pressure that if the film flops, the director may never make another.

Director Peter Bogdanovich had answers to the barrage of questions on the set because he could dip into his encyclopedic knowledge of film. He used index cards to record important data on, and his personal assessment of, every film he saw; between the age of twelve and thirty he accumulated 5,316 of these cards. He went to between six and eight movies a week. His favorites, like *Citizen Kane*, the film that inspired him to become a director, he saw multiple times. He got a job programming films for the Museum of Modern Art, then writing about films for *Esquire* magazine. When he interviewed directors, they were always impressed by his knowledge of their films. Bogdanovich could recite all the credits, recall each cut and camera move. They warmed to him, and he became friends with the most famous directors of the time. He used to go to Times Square and watch five movies a day, then go home and watch more on *The Late Show*. At a film screening, a Hollywood hotshot who was impressed by his writing for *Esquire* offered him the role of assistant director on an upcoming movie, launching his career as a filmmaker in his own right.

His haunting film *The Last Picture Show* was nominated for eight Academy Awards in 1971. The film felt new and old at the same time because Bogdanovich shot in black-and-white when color was standard. He used long tracking shots instead of breaking up important scenes, a result of studying *Citizen Kane* for hours. *The Last Picture Show* broke new ground by using a song score. Period-specific songs were played on radios, jukeboxes and gramophones within the film. It's been done to death since, but never with such subtlety.

It's a lesson in immersing yourself in every aspect of your interest. Know everything there is to know about it. Whether you work in finance, science, teaching or something else entirely, read every book and magazine, go to every lecture and research your subject in every way you can think of. When there is a crisis, you will have a pool of knowledge to dip into.

Quentin Tarantino worked at a video rental store. An obsessive film fan, he watched and discussed with the customers as many films as he could and paid close attention to the types of films they liked to rent. Tarantino has claimed that this influenced his decisions as a director; he has been quoted as saying: "When people ask me if I went to film school, I tell them, 'No, I went to films.'" Both he and Bogdanovich taught themselves how to make films by studying films. Tarantino also used song scores, as Bogdanovich had.

Delve into books, magazines, documentaries, your heroes and your mentors, because these are the gateways to creative opportunities. They will open up a pathway. Study the latest ideas circulating in your field. Immerse yourself, and see where your expertise leads you.

NOTHING IS ORIGINAL. STEAL FROM ANYWHERE THAT RESONATES WITH INSPIRATION OR FUELS YOUR IMAGINATION. DEVOUR OLD FILMS, NEW FILMS, MUSIC, BOOKS, PAINTINGS, PHOTOGRAPHS, POEMS, DREAMS, RANDOM CONVERSATIONS, ARCHITECTURE, BRIDGES, STREET SIGNS, TREES, CLOUDS, BODIES OF WATER, LIGHT AND SHADOWS.

—Jim Jarmusch

Interested? Reinvent something that's already been done on page 50. Not interested? Embrace ignorance on page 95, or be a beginner forever on page 4.

Cross-pollinate

Most of us are alive today thanks to Alexander Fleming. Millions of lives have been saved by his discovery of penicillin and antibiotics. If an antibiotic hasn't saved you personally, it has saved one of your ancestors.

What distinguished Fleming from other scientists was that he thought like an artist; he was more interested in experiments that went wrong than in those that worked. He didn't follow the logical and reasonable path but searched instead for the weird and different. He favored the methods of painters over those of scientists.

In September 1928, Fleming found a fungus killing abandoned bacterial cultures. He was fascinated by the colors and patterns the fungus created. This led to his discovery of the antibiotic properties of penicillin, properties that would change the world of medicine forever. Many other scientists had seen penicillin growing on their petri dishes, but they had dismissed it as a mistake and thrown those cultures away.

Fleming was an avid watercolor painter. He had more affinity with the artists he mixed with at the Chelsea Arts Club than with his fellow scientists. He also painted in an unusual medium, depicting dancers, buildings, battle scenes and other subjects using bacteria, which he created by growing microbes, carefully cultivating the vibrant colors he needed. The fact that they were alive added to Fleming's passion for his work—both artistic and scientific.

When Fleming discovered penicillin, what he had really been looking for was something he could use in one of his paintings, something rare. Fleming spent his life searching for the unusual and the processes that created it.

Many great scientists, in addition to a dedication to their subject, are deeply interested in the arts. Einstein played the violin every day and took his instrument with him everywhere. Darwin was deeply interested in Shelley. Niels Bohr adored Shakespeare. Their broad interest in culture enriched their own subjects.

Innovative companies like Danish hearing-aid producer Oticon appreciate the benefits of cross-pollination of ideas. They discovered that spontaneous meetings were taking place on stairwells in their offices. Employees from different floors were exchanging ideas and information. Oticon widened the stairs to encourage these multidisciplinary discussions. Nokia encouraged their staff to eat lunch in their cafeterias rather than at their desks or outside the office. Sharing diverse ideas leads to bold new solutions.

YOU CAN LOOK ANYWHERE AND FIND INSPIRATION.

—*Frank Gehry*

Find out how Robert Zimmerman used a similar approach to turn himself into the world's most popular singer-songwriter on page 115. Or meet another great thinker who refused to be constrained by the limits of his field—and made us all richer in the process on page 41.

take jokes seriously

When Mark Zuckerberg helped to create Facebook, he wasn't trying to build a global company; he was indulging in subversive humor. Facebook was developed to allow fellow students at Harvard to select the best-looking person from a choice of photos. It caused outrage and was banned by the college, but it was so popular that it crashed the university's servers.

Many of Andy Warhol's paintings started out as a joke. He produced a series of silk-screen paintings of dollar bills in rows and columns: a wry joke about the value of art. Collectors paid millions of dollars for a few dollars.

A joke that launched an artistic revolution was Marcel Duchamp's *Fountain*, which went on to become one of the most influential works of the twentieth century. On a lark, Duchamp submitted a piece of "art" to an exhibition: a porcelain urinal, which he titled *Fountain*.

The piece was never exhibited; the curators refused to display it—but its submission caused uproar. Was it art or not? *Fountain* was thrown away. Forgotten. A photograph was the only record of the original object. The key to its success was that the photo was reproduced in an avant-garde art magazine. The reputation of *Fountain* grew. It was repeatedly reproduced in art magazines and books. Collectors clamored to buy it because of its fame, so Duchamp decided to remake it. There was a problem, though; the manufacturer had stopped producing that urinal. Duchamp had to hire craftsmen to make an exact replica by hand—a delicious irony.

Humor is a bait and switch. A joke is funny because it causes "insight switchover" from a familiar pattern to a new, unexpected one. It is this moment of surprise and realization that triggers laughter. Duchamp didn't intend *Fountain* to become the centerpiece for a history of modern art. He was poking fun at the art world's reverence for traditional techniques. It was only when the art world started taking the joke seriously that he too started to. Spurred on by its unexpected success, Duchamp started an art form known as the "ready-made," an ordinary manufactured object that the artist selected and sometimes modified. Duchamp saw these works as an antidote to traditional, handmade art. Simply by choosing the object, it became art.

Creativity is about producing the unexpected and seeing things from a new perspective. Humor can be instrumental in shifting that expectation.

We often find ourselves feeling anxious, busy and over-whelmed at work. Rather than being weighed down by a serious mindset, what we really need is humor. Humor is a key that opens the door to counterintuitive and subversive thinking. If you've reached an impasse and are feeling stuck, a good joke can lead you to a fresh perspective and spark new insight.

> ONLY THOSE WHO ARE CAPABLE OF SILLINESS
> CAN BE CALLED TRULY INTELLIGENT.
>
> —*Christopher Isherwood*

Inspired? Be mature enough to be childish on page 72.

go from a to b via z

Lobsters hide in nooks and crannies in the rocks on the seabed. They stay in place so long, they literally grow into the rocks. It's worth asking yourself if you might be stuck—embedded in your routine surroundings—too.

One of my favorite assignments is to task my students with exploring a small patch of London, circled on a city map. It takes them to parts of the city they haven't seen. They knock on doors and persuade the occupants to let them walk through their houses and offices. Sometimes I make it harder by asking the students to take a sofa along with them. It changes their perspective of the city. They meet people they wouldn't normally meet, see inside buildings that are normally closed to them. Other things they have done include staging soccer matches with three sides playing at the same time, and using a map of Paris to guide them around New York.

We all develop habits. We walk the same route to the subway, pick up the same paper and turn on the same computer—like robots. We find ourselves behaving automatically. We stop being aware of what we're doing. But to think creatively you must be constantly aware, alive to possibilities of the moment.

Guy Debord pioneered a new way of perceiving the world called psychogeography. Its purpose was to jolt people into a new awareness of their surroundings. To wake them up. Psychogeographers devised situations that disrupted the ordinary and normal in order to shake people out of their customary ways of thinking and acting. The psychogeographer finds different ways to travel and demands that you reconnect with the journey, to pretend you don't know your city, the roads or the buildings. We're prompted to look deeper, with fresh eyes, and act with heightened awareness.

One of my favorite examples of psychogeography was unintended. In *The Art of Looking Sideways*, Alan Fletcher tells of an American explorer who died at the North Pole. His relatives paid an Inuit a lot of money to fly back with the body. The Inuit had never before left the Arctic, so after he'd delivered the body he decided to spend the money traveling around the States. He didn't speak English, though, so at railway stations, to buy a ticket he simply repeated sound by sound whatever the traveler standing in front of him had said when buying his or her ticket. The Inuit randomly crisscrossed the States. Eventually he ran out of money in a small town in Ohio. He lived there for the rest of his life.

If you always take the same path, you will know where you are but you will lose yourself. If you always do the same things in the same way, you will get the same results. In any workplace it's easy to fall into the trap of doing the same old things in the same old way, and ending up with the same results. Change is good, even if it's just changing your desks around. Growth is painful and change is painful, but nothing is more painful than staying in the wrong place. The more often you do something the same way, the more difficult it is to consider doing it differently. There are times when we all have to go from A to B—but go via Jupiter.

CREATIVITY IS THE DEFEAT OF HABIT BY ORIGINALITY.

—*Arthur Koestler*

Discover what George Eliot had to say about repetition on page 119.

never leave improvisation to chance

When Herbie Hancock was playing with Miles Davis and hit some wrong chords, Miles Davis simply played a solo around them. Davis turned the bad notes into good music. He wasn't angry about the mistakes and didn't make Hancock feel bad about himself. The reason Davis was so tolerant was because he was confident of his own abilities, confident he could handle anything thrown at him. This in turn made Hancock feel confident and free to experiment. An improvisational attitude encourages people to be flexible and adapt.

Miles Davis's group made quick decisions under pressure. All jazz musicians improvise when soloing, but Davis created an atmosphere in which his musicians never censured each other's mistakes—errors were simply another, more unusual route. He would even discourage them from practicing—so that a fresh discovery would always be waiting around the corner. This is why, when Davis's band performed, they sounded way better than the sum of their parts.

A jazz band is the perfect model for how any big company or organization should function. In the old-fashioned hierarchical model, leaders are like conductors in charge of an orchestra following a rigid script. People are judged by how closely they follow the script. This instills a fear of getting things wrong, of making mistakes. The world champion boxer Mike Tyson said, "Everyone has a plan until they get punched in the mouth." Most plans get punched in the mouth. Rather than stick rigidly to the strategy, confident leaders see a mistake as an invitation to a new route. They organize themselves so that they can be at their best, whatever happens.

It's a mistake not to make mistakes. The world's best leaders and teams take a more innovative approach. Improvisation is too important to leave to chance.

MORE OF ME COMES OUT WHEN I IMPROVISE.

—*Edward Hopper*

Inspired? Plan to have more accidents on page 82.

reject acceptance and accept rejection

Jonathan Livingston Seagull by Richard Bach was rejected 140 times before it was finally published. *Gone With the Wind* by Margaret Mitchell: thirty-eight. *Carrie* by Stephen King: thirty. *Watership Down* by Richard Adams: twenty-six. *Harry*

Potter and the Philosopher's Stone by J.K. Rowling: twelve. *Twilight* by Stephenie Meyer: fourteen.

What these writers all had in common was a discipline and dedication to sacrifice comfort, to see their projects through. Every time a manuscript was rejected they reworked it—improved the opening line, made the opening more dynamic or added a more satisfying ending. They improved their work and they improved as writers.

No one likes rejection, but everyone, even the great creative thinkers, experiences it. How you respond to it often determines whether your work will ultimately succeed or fail. Rejection strengthens and invigorates the resolve of highly successful people.

Fear of rejection can stop you from putting your work out there. Those rejecting you—art dealers, publishers, promoters or critics—have their own motivations. When a gallery turns an artist's work away, it's often not because the work is poor quality, but because it doesn't suit the philosophy of the gallery or because the style or subject matter isn't compatible with their other artists. Perhaps the prices for the work are too high or too low for their collectors. Maybe the art is simply too large for the gallery. It's not always a judgment about whether the work is good or bad. Great creative people figure out that they have nothing to lose by rejection.

I once bumped into one of my ex-students who optimistically said, "My rejection letters have been more encouraging lately." I'll never forget his positive attitude. It was really touching. Later still I heard he'd had an acceptance letter. Praise and success breeds complacency and mediocrity. Rejection breeds determination. It encourages you to reexamine your work and improve it, to strive to be better.

> I THINK ALL GREAT INNOVATIONS ARE BUILT ON REJECTIONS.
>
> —*Louis-Ferdinand Céline*

Discover the joy of self-doubt and inadequacy on page 29.

be as annoying as possible

In 1729 Jonathan Swift wrote and published a book, *A Modest Proposal*, that suggested poor children should be eaten. Swift was a respected writer of books such as *Gulliver's Travels*, and when he suggested in his new book that Irish parents should sell their children to the rich as food, it was taken seriously by some. The book describes the plight of starving beggars in Ireland and proceeds to observe, "A young healthy child well nursed, is, at a year old, a most delicious nourishing and wholesome food, whether stewed, roasted, baked or boiled." Swift explained in detail why it was a good idea to eat children; he listed recipes, preparation methods for cooking and calcula-tions explaining the financial benefits to the poor. Toward the end of the book Swift gradually introduced the reforms he claimed to believe were the solution, and the reader slowly real-ized he had been provoked.

Swift's book had a profound impact. A sober and conven-tional proposal of reforms would likely have gone unnoticed. Swift wanted to change things quickly. He needed to make an impact and to get his point across to a mass audience. He took a chance. It could have backfired badly, but it didn't.

Provoke a reaction. Provoke change. If you want to com-municate a message, you need to attract people's attention. Otherwise you're talking to yourself. Every creative thinker is at heart a cultural provocateur who wants to change, transform and raise awareness.

Creativity is not for the cautious. It's for people who put their neck on the line. We should not be scared of causing offense; we should be scared of not being heard.

I OBVIOUSLY IRRITATE PEOPLE. I OBVIOUSLY ANTAGONIZE THEM.

—Peter Greenaway

Inspired? Throw truth bombs on page 108.

get out of your mind

Women in a mental institution made Hans Christian Andersen realize he was too sane.

Andersen achieved worldwide fame in the nineteenth century for his imaginative and exotic fairy tales such as "The Ugly Duckling" and "The Princess and the Pea," and his stories continue to be read around the world. They have introduced generations of children to a whimsical world of imagination. Andersen crafted tales and built dreamy, fantastical worlds that were driven by an intuitive common sense.

Tales told by women who had been committed to the local asylum, where his grandmother was a gardener, inspired him. Andersen sat and listened avidly to their improvised tales full of witches, fairies, goblins and trolls. They schooled him in the art of stream of consciousness and improvised storytelling. Imaginative worlds, strange surreal characters and weird situations poured from their unbalanced minds. As Ray Charles put it, "Dreams, if they're any good, are always a little bit crazy." But the women's stories were without form; Andersen combined their exotic imaginations with structured plots. Getting those twin aspects working in tandem was the key to his success.

Many credit Andersen with exploring the subconscious mind decades before Freud's studies, and see him as a forerunner to the twentieth century's surrealist movement.

Creativity requires a mixture of unfettered imagination and practical application; random invention and playfulness held together with an underlying thread. Children and the mentally ill provide 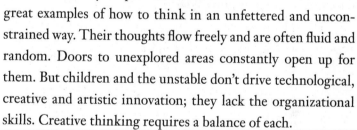 great examples of how to think in an unfettered and unconstrained way. Their thoughts flow freely and are often fluid and random. Doors to unexplored areas constantly open up for them. But children and the unstable don't drive technological, creative and artistic innovation; they lack the organizational skills. Creative thinking requires a balance of each.

Encourage your mind to wander—it will produce remarkable results.

OPEN THE WINDOW OF FANTASY TO KNOW
WHAT REALITY CAN BRING.

—*Raul D. Arellano*

Discover why the author hasn't done any ironing for two years—and why that's a good thing—on page 124.

Stay playful

The most popular TV program of all time had a dynamic birth. Out of the blue, the Fox Broadcasting Company asked a newspaper cartoonist to pitch to create a short animation series for TV. It was his big break. He intended to use the characters from his successful cartoon strip, *Life in Hell*. He discovered fifteen minutes before the pitch that Fox would insist on owning all rights to the characters, and he didn't want to lose control of those ones. He decided not to show the executives what he had prepared and realized that he needed a completely new idea, immediately. In a desperate situation, he hurriedly formulated a dysfunctional cartoon family while waiting in the lobby. He gave them the only names he could think of quickly, those of his own parents and siblings. He won the pitch. It evolved into a half-hour program running every week for twenty-five years—generating movies, books, toys and a pop culture empire worth millions. There has never been a TV show to equal *The Simpsons* in terms of cultural impact.

Mindlessly memorizing information at school was so boring to Matt Groening that he was completely disengaged. He wanted to express himself, so during his lessons he secretly drew instead. The thrill of making something out of nothing inspired him to produce hundreds of drawings. His refuge was the art room. He soon realized he lacked traditional artistic talent, so he incorporated stories and jokes into his drawings to make them more interesting. He explained that cartooning suited people like him who couldn't quite draw and couldn't quite write—so they had to put those two half-talents together to come up with a career. Groening believed cartoons would be his livelihood. His friends had similar dreams too, but one by one they became serious grown-ups. Groening knew he couldn't follow them. He continued to play; he worked as a cartoonist and did part-time jobs to stay afloat financially.

Groening watched the spirits of his contemporaries, who had taken a serious attitude toward their professions, slowly wither and die. Their lives dried up as his blossomed.

Whoever or whatever you do, staying playful is the only way to make the most of the situation. Play can help any field of activity, because through it we discover and explore all available options.

Author and psychiatrist Dr. Stuart Brown spent decades studying the importance of play for people in all walks of life, including businesspeople and Nobel Prize winners. He reviewed more than six thousand case studies that explored the role of play in each person's life. He discovered that lack of play was an important factor in predicting criminal behavior among murderers in Texas prisons. Brown explained that play should be "purposeless, fun and pleasurable." The focus should be on the actual experience, not on competing or achieving a reward.

Play is a catalyst. It boosts productivity and is vital for problem-solving. Play is not taken seriously enough; it is as important for adults as for children. We don't lose the need for novelty just because we become older. We all need to remember that play creates useful and practical solutions. You're a success in your field if you aren't sure if what you're doing is work or play.

> MAN IS MOST NEARLY HIMSELF WHEN HE
> ACHIEVES THE SERIOUSNESS OF A CHILD
> AT PLAY.
>
> — *Heraclitus*

Feeling too old to be childish? Let Frida Kahlo persuade you otherwise on page 102.

don't follow the herd

The Kellogg Company was transformed into a success by a counterintuitive decision by Will Keith Kellogg. In the late 1920s, Kellogg's was one of the competitors in the packaged-cereal market. When the Depression struck, the other companies did the predictable thing: they reined in expenses and cut back on advertising. It was the accepted wisdom. In hard times, most firms invest less in research and development. They try to preserve what they have. That was rational. It made sense. Kellogg made an irrational decision: he doubled his advertising budget instead. The Great Depression was just getting started, but he reasoned that people still needed to eat, and the breakfast of choice for most Americans was "flakes and milk." Kellogg's accountants and financial advisers were pressuring him to make cuts, but Kellogg saw that he would never have such a huge competitive advantage again—and he was proven right, emerging as the market leader by the end of the Depression. Today, statistics show that companies that continue spending on advertising during recessions do significantly better than those that make big cuts. Despite the evidence, many firms continue to follow their emotions and cut advertising in hard times.

Original thinkers are able to tune out their fears, along with the noise coming from the sidelines. They analyze *how* they are thinking as well as *what* they are thinking. This enables them to see these accepted truths for what they are, and to go along with them or ignore them as they see fit.

Try to keep a distance between yourself and the common wisdom. If you clarify your thoughts, you'll have a deeper understanding than those around you. Be prepared to swim against the tide.

Meet three other luminaries who swam against the tide on page 41, page 164 and page 191.

Project yourself into the future

Torrential rain hammers down from permanently dark skies onto a sprawling city of glass and steel. In the decaying streets, all traces of nature have been obliterated. Overhead, flying cars soar between the buildings and a huge hovering airship projects ads for "adventure" in off-world locations. Thunderous sounds rumble as belching mushroom clouds of fire and smoke randomly erupt. Most people have left the planet for an off-world colony, driven away by crime and pollution. A mixture of races mingle in the retrofitted bars, where amid the chaos and destruction the camera falls on a Blade Runner.

Ridley Scott's film *Blade Runner* imagines the implications of cloning and creating artificial human beings—of a paranoid world where searchlights penetrate into every dark corner and the police are omnipresent—the unchecked growth of corporate power as the Tyrell Corporation looms over the city in a giant pyramid. Science fiction asks the question "Will the future be a utopia or a dystopia?" An ideal society where everyone lives in harmony or an entirely dysfunctional society?

The Chinese were world leaders in manufacturing—but they needed someone to tell them what to manufacture. They couldn't invent their own products. The Chinese government wanted to change that, so they sent a delegation to the US to research how the workforce at Apple, Google and Microsoft became so innovative. The researchers found one common factor—most of the workers had been fans of science fiction when they were young.

Science fiction is a combination of rigorous science and unfettered imagination, taking us to places that don't exist. Once you've visited the future, you are less content with the world around you. That discontent drives people to alter and improve, to make things better.

The Chinese had a problem, though: they had banned science fiction during the Anti-Spiritual Pollution Campaign of 1983–1984, deeming it dangerous and subversive. As a result of their research in the US, though, the Chinese switched from banning science fiction to vigorously promoting it. China is now the world's biggest market for science fiction, with the highest circulation of magazines and books.

Google, Apple, eBay, Yahoo and many other tech companies are fascinated by the future. They constantly try to anticipate, envision and shape what's coming.

We all create science fiction. We plan new kitchens, careers and holidays. We see ourselves in them. We visualize them. What would the best and worst be like? We see the events, hear the sounds and feel the emotions.

The ability to project ourselves into the future is one of the key features of being human. Our imaginations are the most powerful tools we have, more powerful than any car, airplane or rocket because it's our imaginations that create the car, airplane or rocket. Imagination has practical benefits—but it needs to be nurtured and maintained. Where are you going? To what extent can you shape your own destiny? Any one of us, at any time, can change our future by asking, "Who do I want to be in ten years?" and "Where's the limit of what's possible?"

CHANGE IS THE LAW OF LIFE. AND THOSE WHO LOOK ONLY TO THE PAST OR PRESENT ARE CERTAIN TO MISS THE FUTURE.

— John F. Kennedy

Not sure? Try living in the here and now instead on page 73.

box your way out of boxes

Asked to write an extremely short story for a magazine? Make a feature of the brevity. Asked to design a building on a steep mountainside? Build out in a way that exaggerates the acute angles. Asked to paint a picture on a curved ceiling split into sections? Michelangelo overcame that limitation when painting the ceiling of the Sistine Chapel. The biggest challenge was fitting human figures into a ceiling crisscrossed by spandrels. The chapel ceiling was a barrel vault, curving downward, segmented by spandrels and viewed from sixty feet below. It required amazing imagination to adapt to the perspective distortion. Michelangelo used the unusual shapes of the spandrels to create a more dynamic composition than if he had been given the freedom of a clear ceiling. He had to design scaffolding built out from holes in the wall rather than built up from the floor. For the first time in his career, he had to use the complicated fresco painting technique. He painted standing and looking upward for months, making the ceiling the most physically demanding series of paintings ever completed. The expanse was huge in comparison to other works of art: roughly six thousand square feet.

Five hundred years later, the ceiling still inspires awe. It's a masterpiece of drama, color, figure, motion and scene. The viewer hardly notices the spandrels because they are so well integrated into the composition.

Search for ways around, under and over barriers. Restrictions force the inventive mind into unique and unusual solutions. Don't dismiss an opportunity that's outside your comfort zone. Practical difficulties can lead to original solutions. Creativity is often a response to constraint. It thrives when there are challenges to overcome.

IN ART, PROGRESS LIES NOT IN AN EXTENSION,
BUT IN A KNOWLEDGE OF LIMITATIONS.

— Braque

More? Make freedom a career on page 191, or discover how to turn a setback into an opportunity on page 106.

to learn, teach

I was taught by one of the most famous artists of all time, the Renaissance master Raphael. There is a direct line of teaching that leads from Raphael to me. I discovered this via a piece of work by the fascinating English artist Tom Phillips; he traced back his artistic connections, and I adapted his findings to my own lineage. When I was at university I was taught by one of England's greatest modern artists, Frank Auerbach, who was taught by David Bomberg; he in turn was taught by the great English Impressionist Walter Sickert. Then an unbroken teaching line flows through famous Romantic artists and French portrait painters, via Degas back to Ingres and Primaticcio, Giulio Romano, and culminating in the Renaissance with Raphael. It's possible to go back even further—Raphael was taught by Pietro Perugino, who was taught by Giovanni Santi, and on and on. Now I am a tutor at Central Saint Martins, not so much because I want to teach but because I want to learn from my students. I leave at the end of the day inspired and brimming with new ideas. Real magic occurs when everyone learns together and is simultaneously teacher and student.

The great German composer Carl Orff composed one of the most famous works of the twentieth century, the awesome *Carmina Burana*. But Orff made a greater contribution to music through teaching. He developed a method, the Orff Schulwerk, which used imitation, exploration, improvisation and composition in lessons similar to a child's world of play. It has arguably touched more lives than all the classical music of the twentieth century together.

Many famous artists, writers, composers and scientists teach. Not just for the money but also to keep in touch with the young and with new ideas being generated in their field. "While we teach, we learn," said the Roman philosopher Seneca. The best way to understand a concept is to explain it to someone else.

The true teacher protects students against his or her own influence. These teachers encourage students to distrust them. They produce no disciples. A creative teacher teaches nothing, but provides a learning environment. The main task of a teacher is to teach students to question everything—including their teacher.

YOU CANNOT TEACH A MAN ANYTHING, YOU
CAN ONLY HELP HIM FIND IT WITHIN HIMSELF.

— *Galileo*

Discover why even teachers shouldn't be experts on page 37.

be an everyday radical

Medical intern Barry Marshall's colleagues watched in horror. He had taken some bacteria from the gut of a patient seriously ill with a stomach ulcer and poured the murky brown soup into a glass. Then he drank it. The potion contained more than a billion *Helicobacter pylori* bacteria and tasted like swamp water.

A few days later, Marshall started suffering from pain, nausea and vomiting. An endoscopy proved that his stomach had gone from being pink and healthy to red and massively inflamed, the early stages of a stomach ulcer. In 1981 there was no cure, but Marshall took antibiotics and miraculously healed himself. He had proved that stomach ulcers were caused by bacteria, reversing decades of medical doctrine that they were caused by stress and too much acid. The significance was enormous: if ulcers were caused by bacteria, they could be cured. It was one of the great breakthroughs in medical history, saved millions of lives and won Marshall a Nobel Prize.

Marshall was driven to do it because, although he and his colleague Robin Warren at the Royal Perth Hospital in Australia had already proved their case through studies of their patients, mainstream doctors were dismissive. They clung to the established dogma that ulcers, which at that time affected 10 percent of all adults, were caused by stress. Marshall had to watch in horror as ulcer patients had their stomachs removed or bled until they died.

The medical establishment believed that innovation had to come from the major research institutions, not a thirty-year-old intern from the Australian outback. A researcher who attended one of Marshall's presentations commented, "He simply didn't have the demeanor of a scientist." Marshall was also up against pharmaceutical companies that had invested millions in products that alleviated the symptoms of ulcers without curing them. The new theory would throw all that profit out the window. Marshall said, "Everyone was against me, but I knew I was right." Eventually the medical elite had to face up to the irrefutable evidence.

Beethoven had to fight against the status quo. He battled against the standardization of musical forms by reinventing the structure and scope of symphonies, string quartets, concertos and sonatas. At that time composers were paid servants, but Beethoven changed that. He demanded and received high fees. He was the first musician to dine with his patrons rather than the servants—and it didn't stop him from being an argumentative dinner guest.

CEOs used to take over a company and steady the ship. Now they disrupt the status quo, set up a new team and bring in new ideas. If you want to transform things, you need to be in a radical frame of mind.

I WOULD SAY ANY BEHAVIOR THAT IS NOT THE STATUS QUO IS INTERPRETED AS INSANITY, WHEN, IN FACT, IT MIGHT ACTUALLY BE ENLIGHTENMENT. INSANITY IS SORTA IN THE EYE OF THE BEHOLDER.

— *Chuck Palahniuk*

Discover another medical breakthrough that wouldn't have happened without upsetting the status quo on page 164.

Make freedom a career

Theodor Geisel's editors bet him he couldn't write a book with a limit of only fifty different words. Geisel, better known as Dr. Seuss, won the bet and in the process produced one of the highest-selling children's books of all time, *Green Eggs and Ham*. Van Gogh used a maximum of six colors when painting. Picasso focused on one color during his Blue Period. These limitations, taken on by choice, helped.

Jackson Pollock's paintings may look chaotic, but they are in fact highly organized. He planned the color scheme for each one in advance, usually no more than eight to ten colors. He used industrial paint, so the colors were ready-mixed in large tins before he started the work. Paint lends itself to hundreds of mark-making techniques: scumbles, glazes, dabs, scrapes—thousands of possibilities. But Pollock used only one technique: dribbles. He used no figurative imagery. He defined clear limits for his work and kept rigidly to them. But within them he worked with freedom. He didn't make rules; they were more like compass points for him to keep his bearings, to prevent him getting lost in a myriad of possibilities. In the 1950s art critics hailed Pollock's huge Abstract Expressionist paintings as revolutionary and unique.

If you have to decide between a good choice and a bad choice, it's easy. When you have to decide between a good choice, a good choice and another good choice, it's hard. Psychologists have uncovered the fact that too many choices, even between good options, leads to decision paralysis. Professor Hazel Rose Markus of Stanford University's Department of Psychology says: "Even in contexts where choice can foster freedom, empowerment, and independence, it is not an unalloyed good. Choice can also produce a numbing uncertainty, depression, and selfishness."

If you work without boundaries, you'll discover what boundaries you need to erect for yourself. Creative people need to work with complete freedom, but, paradoxically, to prevent themselves from descending into chaos they set parameters and limitations within which they work. Complete freedom can be a dangerous and confusing labyrinth for us to get lost in. Work without limitations in order to discover your own boundaries. Once you have worked out the boundaries you need to work within, you can work with freedom.

ART IS LIMITATION. THE ESSENCE OF EVERY
PICTURE IS THE FRAME.

— *G. K. Chesterton*

Inspired? Bring chaos to order on page 136. Uninspired? Try going from A to B via Z on page 168.

try this at home

The following exercises are not designed to produce specific results but to stimulate you.

They're informed by many of the creative people we've looked at on the previous pages.

PICK A FIGHT WITH YOURSELF

For one day, contradict yourself. If you usually get up late, get up early. Ask yourself, "Why do I do things this way?" If you "can't live" without a morning coffee, have orange juice instead. Question the things you do unquestioningly. If you normally work at the computer, work on paper instead. When you are working, work in the opposite way. Be contrary with yourself, all day. Do the opposite of what you want to do. Rewiring your circuitry will give you a deeper understanding of yourself.

THINK ABOUT YOUR THINKING

Analyze the way you think. What was your best idea? Think back to how you had it and what preceded it. What was your worst idea? Did it germinate in a different way from your best idea? Who regularly inspires you? What can you learn from them? What do you enjoy most about your working process? Create a diagram of your thought processes. Make it practical and down to earth, like a diagram of the workings of a car engine. Then study it. Any surprises?

BE ALONE WITH "FRIENDS"

It's hard to be creative without being solitary now and then. The creative people I've known who work a lot with people— choreographers, theater directors, company officers—all need a surprisingly high amount of solitude. Space to think. Sit in a room and let your thoughts wander. Start with a minute, and then build up to ten, then longer. This is the opposite of med- itating: you're not trying to empty your mind of thoughts; you're trying to fill it up. Ideas will start to creep into your mind. Now you're not alone, you have friends. Cultivate them.

LOOK AT THE OVERLOOKED

Many of the creative people we've looked at have been keenly observant. They've noticed something others had missed. While playing with his children in a playground, Walt Disney noticed how many bored parents there were sitting around. "Why isn't there any entertainment here for the parents?" he wondered. He had the idea for Disneyland. Go to a public space and write down twenty observations of people. Study them. What problem are they presenting that no one has heard?

RENAME YOURSELF

Mozart renamed himself almost every week, all his life. He was baptized Johannes Chrysostomus Wolfgangus Theophilus Mozart, but he generally referred to himself as Amade. When he married, he changed his name to Adam, the first man, as a way to declare himself reborn. He constantly altered his name as a way to experiment with different identities. Think of ten new names for yourself. Are they a statement of your beliefs? What do they tell people about you?

THE OBJECT OF THE OBJECT

Gather together a few objects, maybe a pair of scissors, a roll of tape, a stapler—anything handy. Now play with possible combinations. Move them around. See how they might fit together. Eventually they will form a combination that seems right or feels inevitable. You may have invented a new tool, or a work of art—and a new way of seeing.

OVERHEAR OVER THERE

The film director Christopher Guest gets ideas by listening to people. While waiting in a hotel lobby he overheard an inane conversation between members of a second-rate rock band, and the film *Spinal Tap* was born. Sit in a café, bar or on a bus and write down the conversations you overhear. You'll be surprised at the extraordinary nuggets that will emerge.

MAKE A MARK

Sometimes one of my students is burning with the desire to be creative but doesn't know how to start. It may be that the student loves painting and desperately wants to paint, but can't think *what* to paint. Such students are waiting for a deeply meaningful, earth-shattering concept. It never arrives. I tell them to make a mark on a canvas with paint. It might be a slashing stroke. Then make another mark in response. Then another. A conversation begins. Soon they have a painting. The same is true of writing or any field of creativity. Write one word, then another in response. Soon you'll have a story.

About the Author

Rod Judkins is an artist, writer, and lecturer. A graduate of the Royal College of Art whose paintings have been included in numerous exhibitions, he has lectured on creative thinking at Central Saint Martins, University of the Arts, London, for more than fifteen years. His workshops and lectures demonstrate how creative thinking can energize and improve the work of individuals and organizations in any field.

www.rodjudkins.com
Twitter: @rodjudkins
rodjudkins@hotmail.com